SPIRITUAL HEALTH

UNDERSTANDING THE KEY TO SPIRITUAL GROWTH AND THE FUNCTION OF RELIGION

ROBERT M. BAYNES

Spiritual Health
Copyright © 2019 by Robert M. Baynes

Tellwell Talent
www.tellwell.ca

ISBN
978-0-22881-309-5 (Hardcover)
978-0-22881-308-8 (Paperback)
978-0-22881-310-1 (eBook)

Contents

Introduction

This book is the result of more than thirty years of spiritual study and practice. The topics discussed include: how to purify the mind, the key to spiritual growth, the evolution of consciousness, the history of religion, the relationship between science and religion, and the function of religion in the 21st century.

My hope is that this writing will be helpful to anyone interested in spirituality or religion. My intention was to write in a concise, clear manner so that it would also be accessible to people with limited knowledge of religious teachings. My prayer is that the readers of this book will be inspired in some way to lead a more spiritual life.

The book consists of three sections. Part 1 is structured around brief accounts of experiences in my life, and covers a wide range of fascinating topics that impacted me throughout a twenty year period of intense study and practice. I have included some of my own spiritual experiences, and this section culminates with descriptions of two particularly powerful experiences.

Part 2 discusses a theory of consciousness development that attempts to integrate the stages of development outlined by modern developmental psychologists and the stages of spiritual development revealed in the writings of spiritual adepts from many traditions. This section is greatly indebted to the work of Ken Wilber and Jim Marion. It provides an excellent framework to take a look at our evolutionary history and the role religion has played in that process.

The final section is a presentation of spiritual teachings that I believe can have transformative effects and help a person make spiritual progress. It explains the key to spiritual growth and reveals the three most important functions of religion. For the most part this section is inspired by what I perceive to be the core teachings of the Buddha and Jesus. It is also influenced by my own experiences, Jim Marion, Lama Surya Das, Eckhart Tolle, and Irmansyah Effendi.

For the sake of clarity I would like to make clear how I define four words used often in this book. The first two words are religion and spirituality. Using our bones and the marrow within our bones as an analogy...I see religion as the rigid, outer shell similar to bone while spirituality is like marrow in that it is the flexible, inner core of religious expression.

A person can be religious and not spiritual, but their faith will be hollow and lack vitality. Likewise, the growing numbers of people who describe themselves as spiritual but not religious may have a vibrant spiritual life but it can lack direction and consistency.

The other two words are soul and spirit. The analogy of bone and marrow also works well in understanding the difference between these two very important parts of our being. In fact, there is a verse in the New Testament that uses this analogy. It is found in that unusual document called "The Letter to the Hebrews," where it says that "the word of God is living and active, sharper than any two-edged sword, piercing until it divides soul from spirit, joints from marrow..." (4:12).

Our soul is a vehicle for our spirit (which has no form) to experience both physical and non-physical dimensions just like our physical body is a vehicle for our soul and spirit to experience life on Earth. The seat of the soul is the center/front part of our head and is related to the pineal gland and our "third eye." Truly, our eyes are the windows to our soul.

Our spirit or true self resides in our spiritual heart which is located in the area of the center of our chest. Life is a facility for spiritual growth - the growth of our spirit - so we can remember again about our Source and how we have always been Loved completely, to choose Love and rely on True Source Love in every situation, and to then be closer to God. Every moment of our lives is an opportunity for spiritual growth when we prioritize God and God's Love above everything else.

Life is not about developing our soul, it is not about becoming a powerful being that can manifest their wants and desires. In fact this impulse to build up our soul...to be somebody important and special...even if our intentions are good...is detrimental to spiritual growth and is very much related to why we left Home and became separated from our Source in the first place.

I was not brought up within a religious tradition as a child and did not become interested in religion/spirituality until around the age of 21. Like increasing numbers of people these days my spirituality and spiritual experiences have come outside of organized religion, and have been influenced by many different traditions and teachings. That said, I do consider myself a Christian and for several years now have enjoyed attending services with my wife at our local Catholic Church.

My mother is a loving, spiritual person from a Catholic background. Shortly after my birth she began practicing yoga and learning about more "eastern" forms of spirituality. My father is an extremely intelligent and hard-working individual who has always been a wonderful role model for my brother and I. The two of us were raised in a loving and disciplined environment where we were taught to treat others the way we would want to be treated and to be respectful of our elders.

Every loving parent wants their child to be happy and healthy. This book is for my children Ryan James and Megan Rose. Hopefully it will be a resource for them that has a positive impact on their physical health, mental health, and especially their spiritual health.

This book is dedicated to my parents, whose love and support made its production possible.

Part 1

A Spiritual Journey

It's important to live life with the experience, and therefore the knowledge, of its mystery and of your own mystery. This gives life a new radiance, a new harmony, a new splendor. Thinking in mythological terms helps to put you in accord with the inevitables of this vale of tears. You learn to recognize the positive values in what appear to be the negative moments and aspects of your life. The big question is whether you are going to be able to say a hearty yes to your adventure.

--- Joseph Campbell

My mother tells me that I was reluctant to come into this world. Or at least that is the sense she had while enduring a difficult pregnancy. You would wonder why considering the loving family I was born into and the wonderful childhood I experienced growing up in a small town in Canada.

One of my strongest childhood memories may provide a clue. I distinctly remember standing in front of a mirror around the age of seven and while looking at the reflection of my physical form thinking: "That is not who I am." This realization would foreshadow a later tendency to be drawn to spirit rather than the flesh, and to identify with the spiritual much more than the physical.

It was also around this age that I would have an unusual experience. This incident took place during major renovations to our home which included a new basement. One day while walking down the newly constructed stairs to the basement I fell (almost as if I was pushed from the side), and after reaching for a yet to be built railing my body turned and plummeted face up towards the cement floor below.

It felt like I was falling in slow motion and when I reached the floor it was as if I landed on a cloud. I remember being flat on my back on the cold concrete floor and thinking: "I should be hurt, how can this be?" This experience would quickly fade from memory, however; it would come into my mind many times in later years when learning of similar experiences by other people.

Sports were a major part of my life at this time and throughout my teen years, particularly hockey and golf. Schoolwork came easily and I was blessed to have many friends, in addition to having a very good relationship with my intellectually gifted younger brother. Like many people around my age I was influenced by the first "Star Wars" trilogy of movies as well as "E.T." I would have seen these movies sometime between the ages of nine and sixteen, and recall feeling "blown away" by all of them when leaving the theatres.

I also became increasingly interested in health and fitness during my teen years. Around the age of thirteen I read a negative article regarding the effects of drinking coffee and made up my mind I would not drink coffee. I began working out regularly, including periods of intense weight lifting with several of my friends. I never even considered smoking or taking drugs, and was fortunate to have always been repulsed by the taste of alcohol. By my late teens I became convinced it was underrated how unhealthy soda pop was and eliminated it from my diet.

My late teens were also a somewhat difficult time in that I finally accepted the reality that becoming a professional athlete of some kind was not going to happen, and that I had no clue what else I would want to do with my life. My choices were limited by the fact that I was very introverted with poor people skills. I remember taking several long walks to think about my situation and feeling like something was missing in my life but I did not know what. Eventually I decided to enrol in a business administration program at a nearby community college and upon graduation did not enjoy a very brief career in banking.

So I scratched banker off the list of possible career options and returned home confident I would soon find my path in life. It was during this time that a family friend who was a Christian dropped off a movie about the life of

Jesus for my family to watch. I felt a powerful connection with Jesus while watching this movie and at its conclusion had something of a conversion experience. Knowing my mother was spiritual and from a Catholic background I went to her and told her that I wanted to learn more about this subject.

Having many books to do with religion and spirituality she went to them and decided that "The Power of Positive Thinking" by Norman Vincent Peale would be a good place for me to start. I enjoyed the book and was certainly inspired to strive to keep my thoughts positive and to try and maintain a positive attitude (for some reason I found this most difficult while playing golf). More importantly, I became interested in the power of prayer and learning how to pray. I went to my mother for advice on prayer and for another book to read.

The second book I would read on this vast subject would be "Edgar Cayce – The Sleeping Prophet" by Jess Stearn. This book with its account of this unusual person truly fascinated me. Edgar Cayce (1877-1945) was an American clairvoyant who was said to be able to enter into an altered state of consciousness and respond to questions on a variety of subjects. He apparently discovered this ability after a long period of having mysteriously lost his voice and turning in desperation to a hypnotist for help.

The story goes that Cayce was able to diagnose his condition and suggest the treatments that would eventually restore his voice. For years the focus of his "readings" were to treat medical conditions and word of his amazing ability began to spread. Eventually people began to ask him for information regarding religion and spirituality and his answers would continue to amaze. Coming from a traditional Christian background Cayce claims to have been disturbed when the readings began to describe the past lives of the people who came to him for help.

I think back now and realize how fortunate I was to have read this book without any preconceived ideas about the subjects discussed. Even though I was 22 years old at the time I can honestly say I had never given the idea of rebirth a thought. I was able to decide for myself if it was reality or not, having never been told what I should think about it as a child.

I remember thinking that reincarnation made perfect sense and wondered how someone could believe in a loving, just God without an understanding of karma and reincarnation. How else can we account for the massive inequities in people's lives? Why are some souls born into wealth while others starve? Why does one live a long life while another dies shortly after birth?

According to the Edgar Cayce readings the law of karma is stated clearly in the New Testament teaching "what you sow, you shall reap" (Galatians 6:7). There is also an understanding that we are not to judge people with handicaps or hardships of some kind thinking this is a result of "negative karma." There are other possible explanations and the Cayce material says there is an interesting example of this in the Gospel of John.

John 9:1-3 speaks of Jesus and his disciples passing by a man who was blind from birth. The disciples asked, "Master, who did sin, this man, or his parents, that he was born blind?" Jesus answered, "Neither hath this man sinned, nor his parents: but that the works of God should be made manifest in him." So while the author of this story clearly believed people can sin before they are born, in this case the man was born blind so that others might be positively impacted by his miraculous healing. I like to think of people who die young or have severe handicaps as brave souls who have come to help their families somehow learn and grow because of the experience.

The Gospels also make several references to people questioning Jesus and John the Baptist as to whether or not they were Elijah or one of the other prophets reborn (Matthew 16:14, Mark 6:15, Luke 9:8). They knew the prophecy that Elijah would be sent before the day of the Lord. (1) The Gospel of Matthew tells of the disciples asking Jesus about this, "He replied, 'Elijah is indeed coming and will restore all things; but I tell you that Elijah has already come, and they did not recognize him, but they did to him whatever they pleased. So also the Son of Man is about to suffer at their hands.' Then the disciples understood that he was speaking to them about John the Baptist" (17:10-13).

Cayce would remain a devout Christian and encouraged people to read the Bible and to take Jesus as the pattern for living their lives. The Cayce material was my introduction to many important topics which would remain areas of interest throughout my spiritual development. The readings frequent use of the term "Christ consciousness" is one example.

The focus of my spiritual life for the next few years would be: reading books related to Edgar Cayce, striving to keep my thoughts positive and loving, prayer, and taking Cayce's advice to start reading the Bible. Then one afternoon I stumbled upon a television program in which a woman named Betty Eadie was being interviewed. She was talking about what had happened to her after she had died (!) and spoke with such love and sincerity that I bought her book about her experience the next day. "Embraced by the Light" was my introduction to the near-death experience (NDE), and the subject fascinated me.

The NDE has generated much attention since the publication of Dr. Raymond Moody's book "Life after Life" in 1975. Dr. Moody brought the NDE into public awareness and also made the academic world take notice of the phenomenon more seriously. His influence on NDE research continues to be strong, including his description of a "complete" experience with the now famous characteristics such as: leaving one's body, moving through a tunnel-like dark space towards a distant light, and experiencing a life review.

I have read of many similar cases since, but Betty Eadie's description of what it was like to leave her body still touches me the most. She says:

> "My first impression was that I was free. There was nothing unnatural about the experience. I was above the bed, hovering near the ceiling. My sense of freedom was limitless and it seemed as if I had done this forever...My new body was weightless and extremely mobile, and I was fascinated by my new state of being. Although I had felt pain from the surgery only moments before, I now felt no discomfort at all. I was whole in every way – perfect. And I thought, 'This is who I really am'."(2)

Upon reaching the light at the end of the tunnel NDErs usually describe being overcome by waves of the most unconditional love they have ever experienced. Some people report experiencing a panoramic review of their life. They say this life review is like watching a movie of their lives except they also relive the emotions and feelings of both themselves and the people they associated with.

These accounts of life reviews suggest that all of our thoughts, words, and deeds are somehow recorded and that we are accountable for them. How wonderful it would be if everyone believed this and decided that when their time comes they will review a life filled with love and compassion for others.

NDErs who claim to meet a "being of light" during their experience, particularly while having a life review, often say "the being seems to stress the importance of two things in life: Learning to love other people and acquiring knowledge."(3) Another vivid account of a complete experience relates a message given by a being of light:

> "Humans are powerful spiritual beings meant to create good on the earth. This good isn't usually accomplished in bold actions, but in singular acts of kindness between people. It's the little things that count, because they are more spontaneous and show who you truly are."(4)

Some researchers have argued that NDEs can be favourably compared with mystical experiences that open an individual to usually untapped ranges of human consciousness. The result being that NDEs often produce profound aftereffects that can transform the NDErs view of the world and their spiritual beliefs. The most obvious effect is that NDErs usually no longer fear death and are generally convinced that there is life after death.

Like mystics many NDErs say what they experienced is often indescribable and that language cannot do it justice. There are also comparable feelings of a sense of the connectedness of every living thing and feelings of transcendence of space and time. Many NDErs yearn for periods of solitude and quiet reflection much more than in their past history, and most speak of an increased sense of awareness of the consequences of one's actions.

Another prominent researcher named Kenneth Ring has found that NDErs tend to emerge from their experience with a sense of the underlying unity of all religions. (5) Other common effects include a sense of wonder about life in general, greater concern for others, striving to live in the present moment, and increased feelings of reverence for nature.

During this period of study of the NDE I would experience a much less dramatic life change. Sometime after ending my banking career I was asked to return to working at the local grocery store where I had worked in my late teens. After a couple years of hard work at this store it was announced there would be layoffs. I was shocked to be told that I would be one of them.

A couple of days after being told this I was called into the manager's office. I was told that a mistake had been made and that they would like me to continue working for them. I recall being startled to hear a voice in my head say

"NO" and to my surprise immediately declined the offer saying it was time for me to move on.

Thirst for Knowledge

Another common consequence of having an NDE is becoming driven by a quest for meaning and acquiring a thirst for knowledge. My extensive study of NDEs seemed to produce this same effect in me. Suddenly finding myself with considerably more time on my hands for a few months, my study and practice of the spiritual expanded considerably and I loved it.

Actually the next five years would be a wonderful time of spiritual exploration and growth that would include many spiritual experiences. It was not uncommon for me to be reading four or five books on spirituality/religion at a time during this period. Major areas of interest would include: Theosophical teachings, early Christian groups, mysticism, the Perennial Philosophy, Buddhist philosophy, and Hindu/Vedantic teachings.

The "theosophical" type of material (that in retrospect I genuinely seemed guided to read) always had a strong Christian element to it. The tremendous amount of references to the New Testament in these books kept me constantly rereading the Gospels and even more so the letters of Paul. I was intrigued by a reference to secret teachings of Jesus to his inner circle in the Gospel of Mark:

> And he said to them, "To you has been given
> the secret of the kingdom of God, but for those
> outside, everything comes in parables" (4:11).

And likewise mention of teachings only for the spiritually mature in Paul's letters:

> "Yet among the mature we do speak wisdom...
> we speak God's wisdom, secret and hidden,
> which God decreed before the ages for our glory"
> (1 Corinthians 2:6-7).

The meaning of "the kingdom of God" was of particular interest to me since this was clearly a focus of the preaching of Jesus according to the Gospels. I was reading that the inner meaning of the kingdom of God was that it referred to the consciousness of God. And that the key verse to understanding the mystery of the kingdom of God is found in Luke 17:21 – "the kingdom of God is within you."

So we are talking about a psychological level of being where a person has elevated their mind to such a degree that it results in a fundamental shift in how they see the world, themselves, and others. Paul describes the kingdom of God as a state of being where a person has become filled with "righteousness, and peace, and joy in the Holy Spirit" (Romans 14:17).

I began to understand how inspired writing can have several levels of meaning. Taking the kingdom of God as an example, I also believed that it referred to God's Presence in the world as well as our individual connection with the Presence of God. This new understanding allowed me to be able to read the Bible with new eyes, so to speak. Take for instance the famous verse: "Draw nigh to God, and he will draw nigh to you" (James 4:8). I was then able to understand this verse as: "Draw nigh to the consciousness of God, and God's Presence will draw nigh to you." This would become a focus of my spiritual life.

This is also related to another verse that kept coming up in my reading, "Let this mind be in you, which was also in Christ Jesus" (Philippians 2:5). This verse became a focal point of my prayer life and a motivation to strive to keep my thoughts pure. I began to understand that one of the core Christian teachings was that we must first put on the mind of Christ (Christ consciousness) before we can enter into the kingdom of God.

Another important step was to understand the distinction between Christ and the human personality Jesus of Nazareth. One of the Pauline letters makes mention of how by revelation Paul has knowledge of the mystery of Christ (Ephesians 3:3-4). Then in the letter to the Colossians it states clearly: "God would make known what is the riches of the glory of this mystery among the Gentiles; which is Christ in you, the hope of glory" (1:27).

I began to see that the Christ is not simply the man Jesus who lived on Earth. The Christ is the Word, the Logos, and also the Light (or Divine Spark) at the very core of the true self in all of us. The Light within us is the mediator between the Presence of God and our souls, it is the still small voice of conscience that is always trying to guide us to do the right thing in our lives. Jesus was the Christ personified, one who realized the fullness of the Christ, one who came to show us the way and reveal to us our full potential as children of God.

In the Hindu tradition there is a collection of very highly regarded texts called *The Upanishads*. It has been said that *The Upanishads* represent for the Hindu what the New Testament represents for the Christian. In the *Chandogya Upanishad* we are told: "There is a Light that shines beyond all things on Earth, beyond us all, beyond the very highest heavens. This is the Light that shines in our heart" (3.13.7).

During the time I was reading this type of material my brother just happened to notice in the paper an ad for a lecture with a picture of a person that he recognized from the back of one of the books I was reading. He showed me the ad and I felt strongly that I should go to the lecture.

As it turns out the lecture was nothing special and the author was not the speaker, but during the talk I experienced something I had not experienced before. About halfway through the talk I noticed my concentration level was rising and felt very focused on what was being said when suddenly I saw a soft glow of white light around the speaker's head from shoulder to shoulder. I could not believe my eyes and then I looked around the crowd and saw these halos of light around many other people as well. This would become a regular occurrence whenever I was inspired in a group setting.

One of the more interesting things I would learn during this time period was how diverse the early Christians were in their views about their new faith and about Jesus. It seems evident from the early sources that Jesus was a little known Jewish teacher who wanted to reform his tradition, and that his initial group of followers were also observant Jews who came to see Jesus as the Messiah after his death.

This first group of disciples, nowadays usually referred to as the "Jewish Christians," would have seen what they were doing as being continuous with Judaism and continued to have observed important Jewish practices like circumcision, food laws, and festivals. Many recent scholars have emphasized the significant influence that Jewish Christians had on the early development of Christianity, and some have come to the realization that right up to the destruction of the temple in Jerusalem in 70 CE they were the dominant element in the Jesus movement. (6)

Many commentators have also come to believe that the leader of this dominant form of early Christianity was an individual known as James the brother of the Lord. This belief derives from several early sources, but primarily from passages in Paul's letters and from "The Acts of the Apostles." A few of the most convincing of these passages include Paul's mention of James as one of three acknowledged pillars in Jerusalem (Galatians 2:9), followed by his description of another of those pillars (Cephas) having been afraid to upset a group of people who "came from James" (Galatians 2:12), and the portrayal of James having had the final say at the so-called Apostolic Council in Jerusalem (Acts 15:19).

Later Jewish Christian groups, notably the Ebionites, certainly viewed James as having maintained Jewish practices and idealized him as a principal figure in their own histories. Jewish Christianity eventually died out in the fifth century after Pauline Christianity had become the dominant form of the Christian faith. The author of Acts worked hard to try and present the merging of Jewish and

Pauline views as having been smooth and guided by the Holy Spirit but Paul's letters suggest otherwise.

I find Paul to be one of the most fascinating people in the history of religious literature. According to his writings Paul had been a devout Pharisaic Jew who was familiar with the Jesus movement through his involvement in persecuting its members. At some point he had a dramatic change of heart about the new Jewish sect after experiencing what he believed to be a revelatory encounter with the risen Christ. After his conversion experience he claims to have waited at least three years before going to Jerusalem to visit James and Cephas (Galatians 1:18-19).

Sometime during this period Paul understood himself to have been appointed by God to be the "apostle to the Gentiles," and later began his program of establishing Christian communities in cities; staying for varying periods of time while gaining primarily Gentile converts through the preaching of his version of the gospel. Some of his letters to these communities are preserved in the New Testament and are the earliest writings we have about the Jesus movement. Besides the three Pastoral epistles (1 and 2 Timothy, and Titus) which most scholars think were written by a later member of one of Paul's churches, Paul's letters are generally dated in the late 40s and 50s of the Common Era. (7)

It appears evident that Paul was very knowledgeable of both his own Hebrew tradition as well as Hellenistic (Greco-Roman) concepts. It also seems likely that Paul utilized his knowledge of Hellenism in communicating his message to Gentiles, and that his gospel was influenced by mystical beliefs. Although he maintained a reverence for the Jewish scriptures, his letters to his communities demonstrate that he interpreted those scriptures in unique ways to fit his gospel. After his conversion Paul saw the role of Jewish laws as a "disciplinarian until Christ came" (Galatians 3:24), and that those who were justified by their faith in Christ were "no longer subject to a disciplinarian" (Galatians 3:25).

Paul's views toward Jewish laws may have appealed to a Gentile audience (particularly uncircumcised males) but they brought him into conflict with members of the movement who had more traditionally Hebrew beliefs about the law. It is obvious from the letter to the Galatians that circumcision was the primary issue, and that the faction of the movement who continued to see circumcision as necessary was led by James (2:11-12).

Paul's version of meetings with Church leaders from Jerusalem is revealing. He sarcastically refers to "those who were to be acknowledged leaders" as having "contributed nothing to me" (Galatians 2:6). Some scholars conclude from the defensive nature of Paul's writing that after being confronted with Paul and his gospel, the leaders of the movement in Jerusalem were troubled by some of his views and opposed him. (8)

One gets the impression that Paul merely tolerated leaders like James as people given the task of preaching the gospel to the Hebrews while he had the larger mission of bringing the gospel to the rest of the world. The fascinating question for me (as someone who admires Paul despite his flaws) is what motivated him to be able to stand up to the leaders in Jerusalem. We are talking about people who could have been disciples of Jesus and in the case of James perhaps even his brother. I feel Paul was probably driven to a large degree by his beliefs in Hellenistic concepts including allegorical interpretation, and primarily by his mystical experiences.

Several scholars have suggested that Paul was motivated by the Hellenistic ideal of a universal humanity (9), and that even while he was a Pharisee he was troubled by how Judaism would ever fulfil its claims to having universal validity. This view sees Paul as something of a cultural critic who saw the message about Jesus as the answer to the problem and as a tool for radical reform of his culture.

He would have been critical of the ethnocentrism of first century Jews and beliefs that salvation for Gentiles required conversion and the acceptance of covenantal practices. (10) The key for Paul in making his case was in his allegorical interpretation of scripture, the importance of which he makes clear in 2 Corinthians 3:6, "namely, that the letter which kills is the literal meaning, while the spirit which gives life is the spiritual meaning of the text."

Paul combined Platonic notions about flesh/spirit dualism with the Jewish view that the body should not be viewed too negatively. Thus traditional Jewish views about the law, circumcision, literal interpretation, and other matters were associated with "the flesh;" not false but inferior to their superior spiritual meanings. Therefore, Paul was able to use his spiritual interpretations to justify his positions as superior to the people who opposed him. He was able to rationalize that someone like himself who knew the risen Christ could have superior knowledge to someone who only knew him in the flesh.

These dualistic beliefs also relate to Paul's view of the physical body having value as a garment for the more essential spiritual body (1 Corinthians 15:42-50), which ties in with his mysticism. Author and scholar Daniel Boyarin puts it nicely when he says: "The issue is not whether Paul was a mystic but rather what function his mysticism played in the formation of his doctrine and practice."(11)

The mystical experience he describes in 2 Corinthians 12:2-4, which most people take to have been his own, says that he believed he had been "caught up into Paradise and heard things that are not to be told, that no mortal is permitted to repeat." Believing he was someone who possessed this kind of mystical knowledge, combined with his claims of receiving revelations from the risen Lord, would certainly have been a major motivational factor in carrying on his mission despite difficulties.

I would learn of another fascinating group of early Christians with mystical tendencies and more extreme views about flesh/spirit dualism called Gnostic Christians. Our knowledge of these Gnostics was pretty much limited to critiques of their beliefs by early Church fathers until a sensational discovery in 1945. An Arab peasant had found a large red earthenware jar containing thirteen papyrus books that were about 1500 years old. As it turns out they were Coptic translations of still older originals. This Egyptian Bedouin had stumbled upon a collection of ancient Gnostic texts. The discovery was near the village of Nag Hammadi, Egypt, and has become known as the "Nag Hammadi library."

For Gnostics, Jesus is the bringer of secret knowledge that only a select few have the spiritual maturity to comprehend and thus gain liberation from the material world. These Gnostic writings found near Nag Hammadi reveal a wide range of varied beliefs apparently influenced by several non-Christian sources. Scholars have suggested that besides Jewish and Christian sources there were also Platonist, Zoroastrian, and possibly even Buddhist influences as well. These texts are all interesting from an historical perspective, but for me one of them stands head and shoulders above the rest.

The Gospel of Thomas begins with: "These are the secret sayings which the living Jesus spoke and which Didymos Judas Thomas wrote down. And he said, Whoever finds the interpretation of these sayings will not experience death." This text contains 114 sayings attributed to Jesus and is considered so important that some scholars refer to it as "the fifth Gospel."

Many of the sayings have parallels in the canonical Gospels while others more closely resemble Zen koans. Interestingly, there is a tradition that the disciple Thomas was sent East (possibly as far as India) to preach the gospel. Scholars are divided on speculation about the date of the original and generally suggest somewhere between 60-140 CE.

Some of us believe that the community that produced the Gospel of Thomas has a connection with the community that gave us the Gospel of John and the three letters of John we find in the New Testament. Both communities held an exalted view of Jesus as a divine being who came to teach us the liberating knowledge that leads to salvation: "If you continue in my word, you are truly my disciples; and you will know the truth, and the truth will make you free" (John 8:31-32). The Gospel of John also has Jesus say: "whoever keeps my word will never see death" (8:51).

We know from the letters of John that the Johannine community experienced an internal schism that led to some of its members leaving the community (1 John 2:19). Passages from the letters seem to be claiming these secessionists would not confess that Jesus had come in the flesh (1 John 4:2; 2 John 7).

Apparently some of the Johannine community had taken their exalted view of Jesus even higher and had come to believe that he was a completely divine being who had only appeared to be human. Whatever the beliefs of this splinter group may have been, the leader of the remaining community wrote that their teaching no longer abides "in the teaching of Christ, but goes beyond it" (2 John 9).

It is entirely possible that this group who left the Johannine community would now be considered Gnostic Christians and that they either formed or joined the community that produced the Gospel of Thomas. Another possible clue that these two communities can be linked together is the reference in the Gospel of John to the doubt of the disciple Thomas about Jesus having a body that can be touched after his resurrection (20:24-29).

Here are a few examples of sayings from the Gospel of Thomas that I find to be particularly significant:

> Jesus said, "If those who lead you say to you, 'See, the kingdom is in the sky,' then the birds of the sky will precede you. If they say to you, 'It is in the sea,' then the fish will precede you. Rather, the kingdom is inside of you, and it is outside of you. When you come to know yourselves, then

you will become known, and you will realize that it is you who are the children of the living father. But if you will not know yourselves, you will dwell in poverty and it is you who are that poverty." (3)

His disciples said to him, "When will the kingdom come?" <Jesus said,> "It will not come by waiting for it. It will not be a matter of saying 'here it is' or 'there it is'. Rather, the kingdom of the father is spread out upon the earth, and people do not see it." (113)

Jesus said to them, "When you make the two one, and when you make the inside like the outside and the outside like the inside, and the above like the below, and when you make the male and the female one and the same, so that male not be male nor the female female; and when you fashion eyes in place of an eye, and a hand in place of a hand, and a foot in place of a foot, and a likeness in place of a likeness; then you will enter [the kingdom]." (22)

Jesus said, "They who will drink from my mouth will become like me. I myself shall become them, and the things that are hidden will be revealed to them." (108)

The Perennial Philosophy

It became apparent early on in this five year period of study that I was also fascinated by most other religious traditions. I recall that Huston Smith's wonderful "The Illustrated World's Religions: A Guide to our Wisdom Traditions" was an early favourite as a source for information. I was enthralled by the wisdom of Confucius, and awed by the beauty of Taoist teachings. I was entranced by the mystical diversity of Hinduism, and stunned by the clarity of Buddhist philosophy.

When I studied Judaism I was immediately drawn to the mystics. I learned that there was a long tradition of Jewish mysticism that included beliefs in reincarnation. The first known example of Jewish writing that accepts reincarnation (sometimes called transmigration) comes from the "Bahir" in the late twelfth century. (12) However, renowned scholar Gershom Scholem has said that he tends to believe that established beliefs in reincarnation during the middle ages have their roots in an early Jewish Gnostic tradition. (13)

One of the most remarkable periods for Jewish mysticism (or Kabbalah) took place in the Galilean city of Safed in the sixteenth century. Led by charismatic figures like Moses Cordovero, Joseph Karo, and Isaac Luria, Kabbalah experienced a profound transformation. One product of their mystical activities was that "the doctrine of transmigration took on the form in which it had its greatest influence, achieving virtually canonical status among Kabbalists and moralists."(14)

Even the fact that mystical brotherhoods emerged in Safed around charismatic individuals was directly influenced by beliefs in reincarnation. A common notion associated with the doctrine was the idea of soul groups who had incarnated together and shared a common mission. Therefore, this led individuals in Safed and other places "to seek to commune with the souls of persons with whom they had a special spiritual kinship."(15)

Among the major figures at Safed, Isaac Luria has generally been regarded as the most influential, having "produced original mythological doctrines and ritual practices that were of fundamental importance to virtually all Jewish mystical creativity after him."(16) Luria developed elaborate theories about creation and the supernal Adam, soul sparks, levels of souls, and his expertise also extended into the doctrine of reincarnation. One major contributor towards Luria's popularity was his ability to provide his disciples with esoteric wisdom, in particular "his practice of telling every student the ancestry of that person's soul and the transmigrations through which it had gone."(17)

The Hasidic movement that emerged in Poland in the eighteenth century was strongly influenced by the Safedic period in many of their teachings, including their acceptance of the doctrine of reincarnation. Today there are many Kabbalists, Hasidim, and other Jewish people who have been influenced by the teachings of the Jewish mystics on reincarnation. It can also be argued that these teachings have had a direct and indirect impact on many people outside the Jewish tradition also coming to believe in rebirth.

Several scholars, including Gershom Scholem, have noted how Kabbalah was a significant element of the various factors that shaped western esotericism. (18) This influence was probably largely at first through Christian Kabbalah and its exploitation of Kabbalistic ideas. A good case can be made that perhaps the most influential branch of this kind of esotericism directly influenced by Kabbalistic ideas is modern theosophy and its many offshoots.

Scholars have noted how the principle founder of the Theosophical Society, Helena Blavatsky, had her roots in western occultist movements before the later influence of eastern mysticism. (19) Moreover, some scholars agree that her first major work, "Isis Unveiled" (1877) was inspired by a Kabbalistic source. (20)

Due to the eclectic nature of many of the offshoots of the Theosophical Society it can be difficult to prove the influence of Kabbalistic ideas on their doctrines, however; it seems likely that their beliefs regarding reincarnation, soul groups, or twin souls have at least somewhat been shaped (directly or indirectly) by the teachings of Jewish mysticism. The Kabbalists of the past would probably be shocked by how many people (both Jewish and otherwise) they have played a part in helping to maintain faith in a loving God through belief in rebirth.

In my study of Islam I was again drawn to the mystics. The mystics of Islam, called Sufis, have produced some of the most beautiful, God-intoxicated writings and poetry I have ever seen. You could say that in essence Sufism is a path of direct experience of the living Presence of the Beloved through surrender to God. The thirteenth century Sufi poet Rumi is considered by many people to be one of the greatest mystical poets of all time.

The aim of Sufism is to purify the self through love of God and remembrance of God's divine attributes. Ultimately there is the realization that the sense of a separate self is an illusion and that there is nothing except God's Love. And as "the seventy thousand veils of self – illusion, expectation, attachment, resentment, egocentrism, discontent, arrogance – drop away over the years, this becomes one's truth, and only God is left to experience it."(21) The self is extinguished like a moth flying into a flame.

Sufism is said to lead adepts to the heart, and Sufis strive to know the truth through what they call "the eye of the heart." Rumi wisely reminds us that "the only lasting beauty is the beauty of the heart."

About halfway through this five year period of particularly intense spiritual activity I had one of the most incredible experiences of my life. One afternoon I was sitting reading yet another book to do with spirituality when I stopped reading and began to think about why I was so compelled to read all of this material. As I sat there still looking at the page I had been reading my eyes went out of focus. I remember thinking "that's weird." And then two words came up out of the page – "universal destiny" – and moved closer and closer towards my face until I finally looked away. I recall that the effect this had on me was a feeling of joy combined with a sense of finding it almost humorous. Then I sensed very strongly a presence up and to my right that also got a kick out of what had happened.

In my study of the world's wisdom traditions the one that had the greatest impact on me (besides Christianity) was Buddhism. As I read about the life of Siddhartha Gautama and his transformation into the Buddha I felt a strong connection with him in a similar way that I had with Jesus years earlier. The generally accepted dates for the life of the Buddha are 563-483 BCE and it is believed that he was born into a wealthy family in India near the Himalayas.

Legend has it that after coming to understand the inevitability of suffering and death he left his privileged existence to become a wandering ascetic seeking spiritual insight. He is said to have studied with Hindu masters and to have surpassed them all. He practiced meditation and self-denial techniques for many years until sensing he was close to a breakthrough. The story goes that one evening he decided to sit under a tree in deep meditation, vowing to either reach enlightenment or die trying. This went on through the night when:

> "As the morning star glittered in the transparent eastern sky, his mind pierced the world's bubble, collapsing it to nothing; only, wonder of wonders, to find it restored with the effulgence of true being. The Great Awakening had arrived. Gautama was gone. He had been replaced by the Buddha." (22)

The Buddha's message would challenge the establishment of Brahmin priests who he felt placed too much emphasis on dogma and ritual. He quickly attracted disciples who would assist him in preaching his gospel (the Dharma). The Buddha would lead them in these efforts for more than forty years until his death, with his final words traditionally said to be something like "work out your own salvation with diligence and determination."

Just like with Jesus it is difficult for us to know what the Buddha actually taught or if what gets handed down to us is the interpretations of followers. He certainly seems to have had little use for metaphysical speculation, seemingly convinced people should not spend their time speculating about the nature of Ultimate Reality when it is beyond human conception. He is said to have made this point with the famous parable:

> "It is as if a man, wounded by an arrow thickly smeared with poison, were to say to his surgeon: I will not have this arrow removed until I know who shot it, his caste, his height, his color, where he comes from; the kind of bow the arrow was shot from, the wood of which the shaft was made and the species of bird whose feathers adorn it. Verily, before these questions were settled, that man would have died." (23)

He also seems to have stressed that people should not just follow what other people say, but should find out the truth for themselves through direct experience. What can be determined with reasonable certainty is that the heart of the Buddha's message can be found in his Four Noble Truths.

The First Noble Truth is that life is *dukkha*. That is life in this world inevitably involves much suffering and frustration. It begins with the trauma of childbirth, continues on through sickness or injuries, is fed by our fears and worries, emerges through conflict with others, and then finally culminates as the physical body breaks down and dies.

The Second Noble Truth is that the root causes of this suffering and frustration are our desires for personal fulfillment, and the craving for and attachment to things which are by their very nature impermanent. Essentially the Buddha is telling us that most of the suffering and frustration that we experience is self-inflicted. Our selfish desires for fame and fortune, a beautiful body, or a perfect spouse to complete us will always result in dissatisfaction. These selfish desires, cravings, and attachments are for things that are "merely substitute gratifications, futile attempts to compensate for our inner sense of deficiency, whereas our deepest desire is to awaken to our true self."(24)

The Third Noble Truth is that it is possible to reach a level of being where a person is so psychologically centered that they are virtually untouched by the suffering inherent in life in this world. Selfish desires, cravings, and attachments cease to be and a person is free of self-consciousness with its self-interest and self-centeredness. The much loved Buddhist text "The Dhammapada" says that when a person overcomes their selfish cravings their sorrows will fall away from them "like drops of water from a lotus flower." One is able to live fully in the present moment full of love and compassion for others.

And the Fourth Noble Truth is that there is a path that leads to this level of being. This is the way of the Buddha and is known as The Eightfold Path. It reflects the Buddha's instructions on how to purify the heart and mind through a life of morality, concentration, and wisdom. (My interpretation of The Eightfold Path will be discussed in detail in Part 3).

I also love the Buddhist teaching of the four divine virtues. The first two can be linked together and they are **loving-kindness** and **compassion** towards all sentient beings. The third is **altruistic joy** which relates to deriving pleasure from the good fortune of others and the overcoming of envy or jealousy. And the fourth divine virtue is **equanimity**, which is the ability to maintain a calm, even-tempered demeanour no matter what life brings your way.

For the Buddhist these divine virtues and peace of mind can best be cultivated through the regular practice of meditation. Soon after I began to study Buddhist teachings meditation became a regular part of my spiritual practice. The first couple of years of my meditative practice were a real struggle, as I found it very difficult to still my mind. I came to have a great appreciation for the eastern teaching that for someone at this stage the mind is like a wild monkey jumping from branch to branch.

I refused to give up or lose faith that it was possible to make progress in training the mind. At first I would only meditate for a few minutes, but then gradually after several years of determined effort I reached the point where meditating for thirty minutes every night felt comfortable and natural. I was able to touch periods of mental stillness that I refer to as "no-thought." It was at this point where I had several unusual experiences while meditating. For example, one night I was sitting in deep meditation (with my eyes closed) when I saw a scene in my "mind's eye" where I was speaking in front of a fairly large group of people about spirituality.

I felt strongly that what I saw would take place in this life. I remember thinking "public speaking, you've got to be kidding me," because at that time I had a significant fear of public speaking. I also had the sense that what I was saying was closer to preaching than lecturing, and recall wondering how that could be considering the non-traditional nature of my spirituality.

At some point a couple of years into my study of Buddhism I had another unusual experience in a very public place. One day I was walking through West Edmonton Mall shopping for something and with no intention of buying a book when it was literally like I was led by the nose by an angel into a bookstore.

I entered the store and walked directly to a book that was placed face out on a pillar for popular sellers. As I reached for the book I noticed the title was "Living Buddha, Living Christ" and thought something like "well, that makes sense I guess." As I walked to the cashier I realized that I was not familiar with its author Thich Nhat Hanh. Standing in line waiting to pay I turned the book over and read on the back that he had been nominated for the Nobel Peace Prize by Martin Luther King Jr., and that the Dalai Lama and Thomas Merton were among the people who admired his work. I left the store in something of a daze and anxious to read the book.

Thich Nhat Hanh is a wonderful Zen Buddhist teacher who is still going strong today. My spirituality at that time was already essentially a combination of mystical Christian views and Buddhist philosophy, but my belief that these two worldviews were compatible had come about largely as a result of writings from a Christian perspective. "Living Buddha, Living Christ" was important to me in that it served to strengthen this belief but came from the point of view of a highly respected Buddhist teacher. Here is an example of this from the book:

"Our faith must be alive. It cannot be just a set of rigid beliefs and notions. Our faith must evolve every day and bring us joy, peace, freedom, and love...And our actions must be modelled after those of the living Buddha or the living Christ. If we live as they did, we will have deep understanding and pure actions, and we will do our share to help create a more peaceful world for our children and all of the children of God." (25)

I would later read Thich Nhat Hanh's "Peace Is Every Step," an earlier work of his that is considered one of the spiritual classics of the twentieth century. This book helped me greatly in my striving to practice Buddhist mindfulness. Mindfulness is one of the core teachings of Buddhism and tells us that we should strive to live in the present moment.

We are to bring constant attention to our every thought, word, and deed as a means to free us from living in an unconscious manner where we are continually influenced by conditioned thinking that can often have negative results. Many sports psychologists today utilize these kinds of teachings in trying to help their clients to achieve greater results in their respective sports.

About four years into this five year period of intense spiritual activity I would have a wonderful experience. One night while lying in bed in that in-between state of being asleep or awake I was thinking about my passion for spirituality/religion and wondering what I was supposed to do with my life. Then it was as if a thought was impressed in my mind, and it was "I am here to help others lead a more spiritual life." I jumped out of bed with joy and ran to write it down in my notebook. As it turns out that was not necessary because that thought has been burned in my brain ever since.

Not long after this experience I was looking through the spirituality section of a bookstore when I was drawn to the title "Whispers from Eternity." I reached for the book, turned it to look at the cover, and saw the picture of a face looking back at me that I instantly knew was the face of someone who would be one of my teachers. I was so sure of this that when I brought the book home I wrote my name and the date inside of it. So I know that I learned of Paramahansa Yogananda in January of 1998.

"Whispers" was full of beautiful spiritual poetry such as the poem "Make me clean again, Divine Mother":

> "Thou didst dress me in raiment immaculate, and sent me out to play. I wandered away and frolicked among the fruitless trees of delusion. The shadows of the forest of suffering enveloped me. I went out spotless; now I am besmirched with the mud of ignorance. O Divine Mother, wash me in waters of Thy wisdom! Make me clean again!" (26)

Shortly thereafter I read Yogananda's sensational "Autobiography of a Yogi," a book considered by many to be a classic of religious literature. Paramahansa Yogananda (1893-1952) was born in north-eastern India with the name Mukunda Lal Ghosh. His family were Bengalis of the *Kshatriya* caste who were religiously inclined and also relatively wealthy.

Yogananda relates that his mother was very loving and liked to tell her eight children stories from the *Mahabharata* and the *Ramayana*, and describes his father as a strict disciplinarian who enjoyed reading the *Bhagavad Gita*. Early in their married life his parents became disciples of a respected teacher, Lahiri Mahasaya of Benaras, who initiated them in the spiritual practice of Kriya Yoga.

Mukunda began meditating with his mother in front of a picture of Lahiri Mahasaya at a young age. When he was around the age of eleven Yogananda's mother died, and this traumatic event seems to have triggered in him an intense, lifelong love for God as Divine Mother.

Yogananda was a spiritual genius who captivated his audiences with his inspiring and loving personality. He was able to use Christian terminology and quote the Bible when speaking on subjects like avatars, karma, and reincarnation, or while explaining his belief in the essential unity of the teachings of the New Testament and the *Bhagavad Gita*. Yogananda was also adept at using scientific language in his discourses on religion, often using Freudian terms or referring to the findings of Albert Einstein.

I had some knowledge of the *Bhagavad Gita* before my study of Yogananda's teachings, but after learning of his love for the *Gita* I also developed a great appreciation for this remarkable Sanskrit work. The eighteen chapters of the *Gita* come from the vast epic that is the *Mahabharata*, and the *Gita* is generally thought to have been produced between 500-200 BCE. For me the *Gita* ranks right near the top of the greatest spiritual texts this world has produced. According to one translator, the "essence of the *Bhagavad*

Gita is the vision of God in all things and of all things in God."

For the most part the *Gita* is a dialogue between the reluctant warrior Arjuna and his charioteer Krishna prior to a battle for a kingdom. The way I see it Arjuna represents the soul, Krishna is the Light of the true self, and the battle represents the struggle of every soul to find their way to the kingdom of God. Towards the end of their dialogue Krishna instructs Arjuna that:

> "God dwells in the heart of all beings, Arjuna: thy God dwells in thy heart. And his power of wonder moves all things – puppets in a play of shadows – whirling them onwards on the stream of time. Go to him for thy salvation with all thy soul, victorious man. By his grace thou shalt obtain the peace supreme, thy home of Eternity" (18:61-62). (27)

"What you do to others you do unto me," says Christ (Matthew 25:40). And likewise in the *Gita* we find:

> "They who see that the Lord of all is ever the same in all that is, immortal in the field of mortality – they see the truth. And when a person sees that the God in them is the same God in all that is, they hurt not themselves by hurting others: then they go indeed to the highest Path" (13:27-28).

I came to understand that essentially what I was being drawn to in studying all of these different traditions was what has been described as the Perennial Philosophy. The term "Perennial Philosophy" has been around for hundreds of years and was made popular by Aldous Huxley's 1945 book of the same name.

Huxley understood it to be an ancient and universal notion centered around the belief that the "divine Ground of all existence is a spiritual Absolute, ineffable in terms of discursive thought, but (in certain circumstances) susceptible of being directly experienced and realized by the human being."(28) These "certain circumstances" are usually understood to be brought about through disciplined spiritual practices, and associated with the great spiritual teachers throughout the ages and across cultures.

Huxley also believed that according to the Perennial Philosophy a complete transformation of consciousness is best brought about when God is thought of as both immanent (within) and transcendent (without), both personal and supra-personal. (29) At least from the time of Philo (a contemporary of Jesus and Paul) the Jewish mystics have been telling us the same thing.

The Jewish mystical tradition has produced some of the most elaborate theories regarding the paradoxical belief that God can be both immanent and transcendent. Kabbalists reject the notion that the infinite God could be separate from His/Her finite creations. They argue that if that which is finite were distinct from that which is infinite, by definition the infinite would no longer be infinite. Therefore, the finite can be understood as an aspect of the infinite.

Towards the end of this five year period of intense study and practice I was becoming increasingly interested in the field of comparative religion. I learned that this field of study which was once known as "Comparative Religion" or the "History of Religions" was now for the most part known as "Religious Studies." I would also learn that the well respected University of Alberta, which was close to where I lived, had a Religious Studies program. I was convinced that this was the field of study for me and that if I was going to be a teacher of some kind I needed to pursue a degree in Religious Studies.

Higher Learning

I began my university studies in September of 1998, and the next four years would also be an intense period of spiritual study, but from a different perspective. Naturally, I majored in Religious Studies, and fortunately I decided to minor in psychology. Considering the fact I was thirty years old and nine years removed from any schooling I was a little apprehensive at the start. However, I soon realized that I would love all of my religion and psychology classes and that I would do well academically.

The academic study of religion has its roots in the Enlightenment of the seventeenth and eighteenth centuries, but it emerged as a recognized field of study in the late nineteenth century. The German philologist F. Max Muller and the Dutch Egyptologist C. P. Tiele are widely regarded as the field's two founding fathers. Muller's "Introduction to the Science of Religion" (1873) is usually identified as the foundation document of comparative religion. (30) It was not until the 1970s that the field became widely known as "Religious Studies."

I would like everyone who reads this to understand that there is a distinction between the academic study of religion and theology. Whereas theologians are free to participate in metaphysical speculation, the Religious Studies scholar has no choice (as a teacher in a public institution dealing with the human sciences) but to study religion as a thoroughly human activity. (31) The scholar of religion should take the insider's viewpoint seriously, but should be free to theorize as to how and why people become "religious."(32)

A student of Religious Studies attempts to gain some understanding of "religion" in its various forms by viewing it from many different perspectives. These perspectives include but are not limited to: the insider's interpretations, critical views (such as Marx or Freud), psychological perspectives (Jung for example), and sociological approaches (such as Emile Durkheim or Max Weber).

I discovered that I was interested in viewing "religion" from every angle. It was also apparent that I had the most to learn from the sociological perspective. The sociological view sees differing kinds of religions as expressions of divergent societies with their different social ideals and collective values. (33) I needed a greater understanding of cultural context and social influences regarding the people and communities who have produced that which we refer to as "religion."

I enjoyed a course on the New Testament where we studied all of its writings with an eye on the social circumstances surrounding their production. Later there was a course on the early Christian communities where I would develop a greater understanding of groups like the Thomas Christians and the Johannine community.

Likewise, I could not get enough of a course on the history of Buddhism.

I loved a class on the Hindu tradition in which we spent about one month studying the *Bhagavad Gita*. In a wonderful coincidence, the day of an exam on material that included the *Gita* just happened to fall on the same day the movie "The Legend of Bagger Vance" opened in theatres. This is a beautiful golf related movie that was inspired by a novel that was inspired by the *Bhagavad Gita*.

The name Bagger Vance is derived from the Sanskrit word *Bhagavan* which is a title meaning "Lord." So anyone with an awareness of that fact will gain some insight into the true identity of the Bagger Vance character portrayed by Will Smith in the movie.

I was delighted to have the opportunity to take a course on Taoism where we spent a good deal of time studying "*The Tao Te Ching.*" The "*Tao Te Ching*" is one of the most revered texts in Chinese philosophy and is the essential text of Taoist thought. We explored this wonderful piece of writing while paying close attention to its historical context and the cultural influences that helped to shape it.

There was also an opportunity to take a class about Kabbalah where I learned a great deal more about the Jewish mystical tradition. I particularly enjoyed writing a paper called "The Evolution of the Doctrine of Reincarnation in Jewish Mysticism."

In my fourth year, which began in September of 2001, I took a course on the Qur'an. Coinciding with the horrific events of 9/11, I could tell it was a very uncomfortable time for the many students in the class who came from a Muslim background.

A course on Thanatology (the study of death and dying) provided me with the chance to study the NDE from an academic perspective. The paper I would write in this class would be my favourite. It was called "Exploring the Near-Death Experience and its Possible Relationship with the Perennial Philosophy."

First I presented an overview of NDE research, and then described examples of religious, medical, psychological, and sociological views on the experience. This was followed by a discussion on the possible relationship between NDEs, with their similar mystical aspects across cultures, and the belief that there is an underlying unity behind the diversity of religious thought.

Is it possible that some of the shamans and religious teachers of the past either had NDEs themselves or were influenced by someone else affected by the experience? Kenneth Ring makes a provocative statement that relates to this question: "I think there can be little doubt that core NDEs give one direct access to the experiential point of origin of religious faith."(34)

My psychology courses all proved to be enlightening. While I certainly wanted to learn more about Freudian psychoanalytic theories I discovered that I was also interested in developmental psychology and social psychology. I was also very much drawn to the major figures in humanistic psychology like Carl Rogers and Abraham Maslow.

Rogers is known for his belief in the potential for positive, healthy growth in people which he referred to as self-actualization, as well as his innovative approaches to therapy. Maslow was also interested in self-actualization and spent most of his career examining the qualities of people who seemed to be the most fully functioning and well adjusted as they proceeded through life. Some of the characteristics of self-actualizers that Maslow found are: accepting of themselves and others, they have sharp focus and can quickly detect distorted perceptions, they have an appreciation for life, and they are often independent thinkers.

An example of a psychological theory that I found especially interesting and relevant to my interests is the theory of cognitive dissonance. Essentially cognitive dissonance is a state of psychological tension where a person experiences discord because of inconsistencies in their thoughts. One example would be a person who continues to smoke when they are aware of how dangerous it is to their health. Another example would be when an individual coming from a religious upbringing where they were taught that the Earth was 6000 years old discovers the overwhelming evidence that the Earth has been around for something like four billion years.

Sometime during my first year of university I stumbled upon a PBS program where Bill Moyers was doing a brilliant job of interviewing an older gentleman about mythology. It did not take long in watching this program to realize that the man he was interviewing would be another one of my teachers.

The man's eyes lit up as he eloquently discussed topics of interest to me like mythology, religion, spirituality, and psychology. As it turns out this was a replay of a popular PBS series called "The Power of Myth" that originally ran in 1988, and the man being interviewed was an influential figure in the history of comparative religion.

Joseph Campbell (1904-1987) was an extraordinary man who touched the lives of countless people through his personal relationships, writing, teaching, and interviews. He possessed stunning intellectual abilities as well as the heart of a poet. Campbell came from an upper class Catholic background and was fortunate to be able to travel the world and encounter many influential people.

Just a few of these experiences that I find of interest include a 1924 family vacation to Europe where on a steamship voyage to England he would become friends with a young Indian man named Jiddu Krishnamurti. Krishnamurti would later be seen as one of the more influential spiritual teacher/philosophers of the twentieth century.

A 1932 road trip to California would result in his becoming friends with John and Carol Steinbeck. In 1934 he was offered a position as a professor at Sarah Lawrence College where he would teach for 38 years. In 1941 he attended a lecture by Heinrich Zimmer who would ignite in him a passion for Hindu philosophy, and who would also become a friend and mentor. And in 1953 he was invited to the Swiss home of the brilliant Carl Jung for an opportunity to sit and discuss a variety of subjects.

Later in life he would become friends with filmmaker George Lucas, who has said that the work of Joseph Campbell was an influence on the "Star Wars" movies. I have heard Lucas refer to Campbell as his Yoda. Then it came about that Bill Moyers would interview Campbell for a PBS series and that the bulk of the interviews would take place at Lucas' Skywalker Ranch in August 1985, and August 1986. The PBS series would prove to be very popular and one of its executive producers has remarked: "It is amazing how many people mention the series as one of the great television experiences of their lives."(35)

Joseph Campbell inspired me in many ways. He was someone who truly seemed to be able to joyfully participate in the difficult process that is life in this world. I love how he viewed life as an exciting spiritual adventure most fully experienced when people allow themselves to be transparent to the transcendent. Here are a few Joseph Campbell quotes from the book "The Power of Myth" that I like:

> "We have come forth from the one ground of being as manifestations in the field of time. The field of time is a kind of shadow play over a timeless ground." (p.64)

> "If you realize what the real problem is – losing yourself, giving yourself to some higher end, or to another – you realize that this itself is the ultimate trial. When we quit thinking primarily about ourselves and our own self-preservation, we undergo a truly heroic transformation of consciousness. And what all the myths have to deal with is transformations of consciousness of one kind or another." (p. 154-155)

> "All of the references of religious and mythological images are to planes of consciousness, or fields of experience that are

potential in human spirit. And these images evoke attitudes and experiences that are appropriate to a meditation on the mystery of the source of our own being." (p. 207)

It was about midway through my university studies when one night while studying I was struck by a most humbling thought. This thought literally stopped me in my tracks, and it was: "The more I learn, the more aware I become of how little I know."

It was also around this time that I was in a bookstore and was drawn to a book called "A Brief History of Everything" by Ken Wilber. Wilber is an interesting integral thinker who has helped me to see "the big picture." He helped me to "pull back the lens" and look at my studies and my life from a wider, deeper point of view.

I like Wilber's theory that there are basically four quadrants of the Kosmos: 1. The interior-individual/intentional/subjective dimension. Chiefly concerned with self and consciousness; an example of an influential thinker in this realm is Carl Jung. 2. The exterior-individual/behavioural/objective dimension. Its area of study is the brain and organism; and a great thinker in this realm is B. F. Skinner. 3. The interior-collective/cultural/intersubjective dimension. Chiefly concerned with culture and worldview; one example of a great thinker in this realm is Max Weber. 4. The exterior-collective/social/interobjective dimension. Its concern is with social systems and environment; an example of an influential thinker in this realm is Karl Marx.

Therefore, for someone with an integral outlook it is possible to admire both Joseph Campbell and Michel

Foucault, the Buddha and B. F. Skinner, Jesus and Einstein, and so on. In a similar vein, it is easy for an integral thinker to see the strengths and weaknesses of typical "conservative" and "liberal" approaches to living in the world.

For example, when it comes to the cause of human suffering, liberals tend to believe in exterior causes and recommend exterior social interventions; whereas conservatives tend to believe in interior causes and recommend a need for family values, individual responsibility, etc. (36) An integral approach recognizes the equal importance of both the interior and exterior dimensions of reality.

Wilber would also help me to be better able to articulate my belief that the relationship between science and religion is ultimately one of integration, with both attempting to explore different aspects of reality. This view sees reality as "a rich tapestry of interwoven levels, reaching from matter to body to mind to soul to spirit."(37)

Each successive level both transcends and includes the "lower" levels, and can be seen to correspond with a specific branch of knowledge. Thus, physics deals with matter while biology studies vital bodies. Psychology and philosophy are primarily concerned with the mind. Theology attempts to study the soul and its relationship to God. And mysticism explores "the formless Godhead or pure Emptiness, the radical experience of Spirit."(38)

Spirit is not seen as being above nature, but rather as a sustaining force that is interior to nature. Likewise, this perspective does not see science as inherently inferior to religion, but rather as intimately connected operations in a search for truth. The integrative approach sees mature forms of science and religion both seeking to probe "deeper into the fathomless unity that underlies all the complex patterning of an ultimately mysterious universe."(39)

Modern physicists have struggled with the problem of paradoxical findings in their research, with the classic example being how light can appear to be both wave and particle. These struggles relate to something else modern scientists and the great religious thinkers have in common: the inadequacy of language to express themselves. Mystics from around the world have struggled with the realization of how their encounters with the inner dimensions of reality transcend ordinary language.

Furthermore, it must be added that "every consistent theology sooner or later recognizes the utter inadequacy even of our loftiest religious labels for ultimate reality."(40) So while some people have argued that all language is metaphor, a mature and lasting relationship between science and religion at least requires the recognition that "theological language is always tentative and metaphorical."(41)

This leads to the point that for religion to be a compatible partner with science it must accept the truth of an old Earth and the fact of evolution. The integrative approach accepts this and understands creation to be a dynamic process of movement and unfoldment.

The integrative point of view would argue that the evolutionary process may very well "be the expression of a divine creativity manifesting itself in a manner that allows for endless diversity and particularity."(42) Many of us see this divine creativity in the awesome beauty and complexity of nature, the elegance of higher mathematics, or the sublime productions of a Bach or Beethoven.

By the end of my third year of university things were going very well and I had won a couple of scholarships. I remember that I could almost literally feel my mind expanding, and I recall thinking that "the brain really is like a muscle." I was starting to believe that not only would I go on and work towards a Ph.D., but that I would eventually revolutionize the field of Religious Studies in some way. So you can see that there was a certain amount of intellectual pride, and looking back now I can also see that in the years leading up to university there was some spiritual pride as well.

In those years I took some pride in my healthy lifestyle and my mystical knowledge. This was fed to a degree by the spiritual experiences I was having and by the fact I was also very sexually pure. I can see now that I was sexually repressed and took pride in it because of a distorted/negative view of sexuality.

This mental/spiritual discipline gradually broke down through my university years. I had always been very attracted to women, and while at university there was no shortage of intelligent, beautiful women. At some point I also stopped meditating and my prayer life became less meaningful, to the point of feeling rote.

Towards the end of my fourth year I could feel that I was mentally burning out. I was so tired of reading, studying, and thinking. I did not work out much during my university years and my energy level had dropped. The guilt and shame that came from dealing with my sexual repression was eating me up. I was so ready to be done when I wrote that last exam.

Darkness then Light

I walked out of university with degree in hand one confused individual. I was mentally burnt out just months away from being places mentally I had never been before. Spiritually I was low, just a few years removed from wonderful spiritual experiences. There was a fair amount of student debt and no foreseeable career. It felt like being lost in the wilderness with no idea what direction to take or what lay ahead. The next six years would prove to be very difficult.

One of the few things clear to me was that I was not meant to be a university professor. I could not bring myself to read anything for months. Eventually I made myself start reading again, but if the book had anything to do with spirituality it would take me a long time to get through it. All I could manage for work was a stint helping UNICEF with their Christmas campaign and to work part-time with my wonderful uncle at a job that required little thinking.

About a year and a half into this difficult period I received a call from an old friend who had recently bought a small produce company asking me if I would help him out for awhile. The work I would do was physically demanding but I felt good about the product and I liked the people I worked with so I asked to stay on full time. There were times this job would leave me so physically drained that I considered doing something else, but on some level I felt I needed to stick with it for some reason. The combination of this very physically tiring work with my inner sense of almost being cut off from God, cut off from that which inspires me, left me feeling like a dead man walking.

I became more and more disconnected from my emotions and experienced periods of mild depression. Lower back pain was adding to my misery. Spiritually there was no progress and just about the only thing that resonated with me was the teaching of The First Noble Truth. This would go on for years, it was agonizing and frustrating.

Fortunately there were the joyous occasions of the births of two beautiful nieces during this period to help get me through it. There was also a modest amount of success playing tournament poker. Competing in poker tournaments gave me an activity that I could be both enthusiastic about and find intellectually stimulating. I was also fortunate to be a calm, steady person by nature. I suspect few people had any idea what I was going through, and I can imagine that for more outgoing, emotional, artistic types of people the highs and lows are much more pronounced.

Life felt like a grind, and I kept grinding away determined not to give up, when finally toward the end of 2007 there was some relief. I noticed my people skills were improving, and I can look back now and see that I was becoming less self-conscious. In the spring of 2008 there was an indication that the influence of the ego was fading. I was talking to a co-worker about some trouble I was having with my eyes being red and irritated when he blurted out, before his brain could filter it, a very negative and honest view of how I looked. This was no big deal except for the fact that I noticed that I had absolutely no defensive reaction to it whatsoever.

I began to sense it was time to make an effort to return to a life of spiritual study and practice. I asked my parents if I could move out to their place by a lake far away from the city. I would spend the next five months living in a trailer and having a one hour drive to work five days a week.

Apart from work this would be a time of quiet contemplation and solitude in a peaceful lakeside setting. I began to read the New Testament again for the first time in years, and also began to find books on spirituality that were just what I needed. I was determined to start meditating again every day, although I found that I was right back to where I was when I first began the practice with my mind jumping around like a wild monkey.

The first book that would help me to come out of this difficult period was "A New Earth" by Eckhart Tolle. Oprah Winfrey had picked this book for her book club and this made me think it must be something special. It is. Tolle is highly intelligent, deeply insightful, and writes with a remarkable clarity. Tolle's goal seems to be to help stimulate an "awakening" in individuals that will lead to a transformation of consciousness. Keys for Tolle are being aware of how our "egoic self" influences our lives, and striving to live in the present moment.

For Tolle the ego is pathological and we need to be constantly aware of its negative influence on our thoughts and emotions. He writes, "Rather than being your thoughts and emotions, be the awareness behind them."(43) The ego is wrapped up in our physical and psychological form and plays roles to try and define itself with thoughts like "my illness," "my greatness," "my wealth," "my bad luck," and the like. Depending on the individual, these thoughts can lead to a mental conception of being either inferior or superior to others. My favourite quote from the book is:

> "But you cannot be more than you are because underneath your physical and psychological form, you are one with Life itself, one with Being. In form, you are and will always be inferior to some, superior to others. In essence, you are neither inferior nor superior to anyone. True self-esteem and true humility arise out of that realization." (44)

I would then finally read his earlier bestseller "The Power of Now." I found this book to be even more lucid than "A New Earth" and an excellent presentation of the importance of living in the "Now." It is written in a question and answer format reminiscent of a book by David Godman on the teachings of Sri Ramana Maharshi called "Be As You Are."

Tolle is clearly influenced (in wonderful ways) by Buddhist philosophy, Sri Ramana Maharshi, and Krishnamurti. He reminded me of the importance of practising mindfulness and of an old saying that I have always liked: "Learn from the past, plan for the future, live in the present moment."

Tolle's books were definitely helpful but I still felt cut off from my emotions and from God. I was to the point where I was willing to try anything to remedy the situation. One afternoon I noticed an ad in a small town paper for a place that offered services like aura cleansing and reiki. I felt that I should give it a try, and I am sure glad that I did. The woman who operated the shop is a beautiful person who is gifted spiritually and has significant psychic/healing abilities. I refer to her as my "energy healer." It was also nice to have someone to talk to about my frustrations of the past six years.

The work that she did on my body was definitely helping, especially in relieving back pain. My "energy healer" told me that the energy around my head was good but down around my hips she described me as "being stuck." The heat that came from her hands while she worked on me was amazing. One day I mentioned I was thinking about trying past life regression therapy and she encouraged me to give it a try.

I had been fascinated by the work of past life regression therapists since my late twenties, especially the work of Brian Weiss and Michael Newton. I felt like I had nothing to lose and that I had reached a point where I had little fear of anything, so I found a nearby therapist who I sensed was a spiritual person. My session with this therapist turned out to be revealing for unexpected reasons.

In our preliminary discussion she made the astute observation that she felt that I had "gone from my heart to my head" in my university years. There was no past life information, in fact I was not even able to relax much less fall into a deep hypnotic state. However, I did discover that there was still fear in me. As soon as I sat in her chair I noticed I was feeling a tremendous amount of anxiety and that I could physically feel it in my chest area.

I decided that this type of therapy was not what I needed and that I should focus on the energy work. After one session with my "energy healer" she gave me a card of someone who had helped her years ago. She did not give me any information about this person, but I trusted her and arranged an appointment. My session with this man would prove to be very interesting.

I will refer to him as a "clairvoyant" although he may not like that title. He must be one of the most down to earth, tough talking clairvoyants to ever walk the planet. He quickly identified me as a "violet/blue type of person" and was very blunt in his assessment of my weaknesses. When our discussion came to the subject of fear I would have a powerful experience that to this day I cannot explain.

He was telling me that my fear was not of being inferior but rather was a fear of superiority. I recall finding whatever he was saying to be profoundly true when it was like a lightning bolt struck my heart. It felt like I was thrown back in my chair and then tears started pouring from my eyes. I immediately put my head down and covered my eyes for I had not cried in years.

I left his office wondering what that was all about, but sensing it was a positive development. Before going to university I was someone who would tear up if I saw people or animals suffering or in distress of some kind. After this session with the "clairvoyant" this tendency began to return. I do not understand what happened to me in that session but the result seemed to be that my heart was opened up again in some way. After that event my head began to clear and I began to make progress meditating.

Shortly thereafter I would find a book that would also have a profound impact on me. One day while looking on Amazon for any new books by Ken Wilber I noticed on the side of the screen the title of a book related to the work of Wilber called "Putting on the Mind of Christ." I was immediately drawn to this title since it described what had been one of the main focuses of my spiritual life. After reviewing it I sensed strongly this was a book that I needed to read.

The author of this remarkable book is Jim Marion, a former Catholic monk. Marion would remind me about and confirm my long held beliefs in the teaching of the kingdom of God, the meaning of Christ, and the compatibility of a Christian faith with beliefs in karma and reincarnation. He also opened my eyes to an aspect of Ken Wilber's work that for whatever reason had never been clear to me. This involves a theory of consciousness development that builds on the earlier works of Sri Aurobindo and the brilliant philosopher Jean Gebser.

This theory integrates writings by saints and sages across cultures regarding stages of spiritual development with the psychological stages of development outlined by modern developmental psychologists. What Marion does is describe this path of consciousness development from a Christian perspective.

He also had the courage to include his own experiences, both positive and negative, as he made his way along his own path. This inclusion of personal material helped me to understand that my experiences of the past six years or so had been a part of the process of my own spiritual evolution. Because my head was not yet clear while reading this book I was unsure where I was on the path, but I could see again that there was light at the end of the tunnel.

Marion gave me hope that I would emerge from this difficult period transformed in a positive way, and he reminded me that the Light at the end of the tunnel was my hope. I felt encouraged to push on in my spiritual efforts and to believe that a breakthrough was going to happen eventually. I moved into an apartment close to work with a renewed determination to "put on the mind of Christ" through disciplined spiritual practice and faith in Christ.

The next couple of months were a time of spiritual renewal, with my head continuing to clear and significant improvement in my meditative practice. I was able to meditate for longer periods of time and to once again experience the peace that comes from resting in no-thought. These experiences of no-thought would come near the end of a meditation session until one night in early December, 2008. On this night I sat down on the end of my bed to meditate and I was instantly at no-thought. This had never happened before and I knew that I was close to a breakthrough of some kind.

About a week later I would have an incredible dream, a dream that I know with every fibre of my being was much more than a dream. I dreamt that a young red-headed boy was walking towards me and that as he approached his face became more and more menacing. As he grew near his eyes turned red and the scene became so frightening that normally I would have awoken with my heart pounding. Not on this night. I was completely at peace and felt nothing but love and compassion for this boy. At some point I noticed I was seated in the lotus position like a yogi.

I intensely stared this boy in the eyes until he began to move away. As he retreated his face began to soften and his eyes turned blue, and then he showed signs of fear before fading away.

The next day after work I phoned my mother wanting to tell her about this dream. After relating the dream and telling her about my recent experiences meditating I recall telling her how strongly I felt that something was happening with me. I remember saying in this conversation that I sensed I was near to a profound shift in consciousness. And as it turns out the dream was a precursor for the most incredible spiritual experience of my life.

That night (Dec.12) I watched the movie "Batman Begins" after two people at work had encouraged me to watch it earlier that day. I found the movie somewhat inspiring and after putting it away I felt a strange ripple of emotion in my heart area like nothing I had ever felt before. I did not think too much of it and decided to go to my room and do some exercise. As I began to go down on the floor to do some abdominal crunches tears began flowing out of my eyes. Since I was not crying I knew something unusual was happening and instinctively went flat on my back with my arms out to my sides. What happened next is very difficult to describe.

My back would arch and I was moaning almost like I was struggling for breath. If I had not been so well prepared for this moment including the dream the night before I would have thought I was dying. Instead, on some level I knew I would not die and there was almost an underlying sense of joy. I spoke to God, saying "take me Lord, I am ready," and at the most agonizing point I prayed "Thy will be done." Gradually the experience eased and I was enveloped by the most wondrous feeling of peace. Truly, this was a peace "which surpasses all understanding" (Philippians 4:7).

This perfect peace was mixed with a sense of awe and wonder, and an awareness of the fact there was no thought, no more mental chatter. I never wanted to get up off that floor. I have no idea how long this experience took place because there was no sense of time. To this day I no longer experience unwanted mental chatter and can go to no-thought at any time and experience the peace that comes from a perfectly still mind. It is glorious and I am so grateful.

I realized the best way I can describe what I experienced that night was that, metaphorically speaking, I was on the cross. My body was reacting as if it was on the cross but I was almost completely spared the pain (thank you Jesus). I believe what essentially died (or was crucified) that night was the egoic self, and I now believe that in some way the ego is the source of unwanted mental chatter like negative thoughts and hurtful thinking. A line of Paul has resonated with me in a powerful way since that day: "I have been crucified with Christ; and it is no longer I who live, but it is Christ who lives in me" (Galatians 2:19-20).

I was in and out of a state of bliss for days. I felt a sense of psychological wholeness that was truly wonderful (since that time I have had the tendency to use the words wonderful and beautiful a lot). About a week later I would have another unusual experience. I awoke wide awake very early that morning feeling determined and focused. As I was taking a shower inspiration came suddenly, and soon

I was at my desk writing an outline for a book with three sections that I felt I needed to write (this is that book).

Then on December 24, I would have a completely unexpected experience, this time at work in front of co-workers. I was feeling emotional all that morning and my head felt strange when it hit me. I was walking toward the desk to get some paperwork when I started to feel very strange and my eyes filled with tears. I took the paper and began walking towards the receiving area but I did not get very far. It was like I was being overcome by a powerful force or field of energy. First I was bent over, then on my knees with my chest heaving for air, and then flat on my back on the warehouse floor.

What I experienced then was similar but different to the experience twelve days earlier. There was not the sense of something dying, instead it was like an intense energy going through my body. I felt a tingling sensation throughout my body and despite the fact I did not feel any pain my body was almost reacting as if it was on fire. I could not stop myself from yelling out loud, and then after one very loud yell my body went limp. I staggered to the bathroom to compose myself wondering why this had to happen at work.

I went to speak with my three co-workers who had witnessed this unusual scene, concerned about what effect it may have had on them. I was pleasantly surprised by their reactions. First, a gifted young man who I had some conversations with about spirituality approached me with tears in his eyes. He told me it looked like I was experiencing a combination of joy and anguish, and I sensed strongly that he knew what he had seen was a spiritual thing.

Next a man about my age who I had worked with for years came over and wanted to talk to me. He told me that he used to be very religious and when he was in church and really feeling touched he would get a funny feeling across his face. He said that he experienced that same feeling while I was on the floor. And finally, a young man with a great sense of humour who I had only worked with for a short time joked that he liked to throw himself on the floor and yell every once in a while too.

That night I felt completely "wiped out" and excused myself from Christmas celebrations to go to bed early. The next morning I felt incredible. The feeling of peace was even more complete and so was my sense of psychological wholeness. I believe this experience was a powerful encounter with the Holy Spirit.

The dominance of the egoic self had come to an end and the Holy Spirit was essentially cremating its remains. The scriptural verse that resonated after this experience was from the Gospel of Matthew, which has John the Baptist saying: "I baptize you with water for repentance, but one who is more powerful than I is coming after me...He will baptize you with the Holy Spirit and fire" (3:11).

My experiences of the past twenty years began to become clear to me and everything felt integrated. The past six years had brought me to the point where the walls of pride that the egoic self builds up around itself began to come tumbling down exposing the ego to the Light. There was a significant decrease in negative thoughts, guilt, judging, and egotistical thinking. There was also a gradual unfolding of love and compassion for everyone.

For several months life was wonderful and I began to believe I had reached the point where helping others to grow spiritually should be my focus in life. However, it soon became apparent that there was still work to do... selfish desires and sexual urges had resurfaced and I began to search for someone to help me with this issue.

Shortly thereafter I was guided to the website of a woman who worked in Edmonton as a "dakini" and energy healer. I had many unusual and amazing experiences with her that brought mixed results. But one day in her office I was drawn to a little card that had the title "Open Heart Prayer," and that moment would lead me to the teacher who could open my eyes to see how far I still had to go spiritually.

This spiritual teacher named Irmansyah Effendi would help me to realize that I actually knew very little about the key to my spiritual growth...my spiritual heart...and show me how to let God's Love open and cleanse my heart. In many ways my spiritual journey had just begun...

Part 2

The Evolution of Consciousness

Little by little, wean yourself.
This is the gist of what I have to say.
From an embryo, whose nourishment comes in the blood,
move to an infant drinking milk,
to a child on solid food,
to a searcher after wisdom,
to a hunter of more invisible game.

--- Rumi

Before getting into a discussion about the function of religion and the key to spiritual growth let's step back and take a look at our evolutionary history. We need to know where we have come from to better understand where we are going, and to learn from our mistakes.

We are complex, multidimensional spiritual beings living in a complex, multidimensional universe. Therefore any attempt at a theory of consciousness development has its limitations. This section outlines a theory of nine levels of consciousness that follows in the footsteps of Jean Gebser, Ken Wilber, and Jim Marion.

This theory is the best framework that I know of to both gauge our own development as well as the evolution of the human race as a whole. Wilber warns us that these nine levels should not be viewed as neat little boxes, these levels or stages of development have some overlap and could be broken down into many substages.

Also, human beings progress along many streams of development such as psychosexual development, moral development, and emotional development. This theory of consciousness development is essentially dealing with cognitive development.

It is also important to understand that this is not a linear process, human development involves many peaks and valleys. For example, a person can be at a high level of cognitive development while also having a low level of emotional development and psychosexual issues.

Marion makes the important point that "we can 'repress' parts of our consciousness that we don't like (usually sexual and aggressive feelings) and these parts of ourselves can remain 'stuck' at the lower levels (where they drain our energy so much that they, unless cleared up later, can prevent our advance to the highest spiritual levels)."(1)

Sexual repression and distorted, unhealthy views regarding sexuality have been common problems throughout the history of religion. These negative views of what should be seen and experienced as a sacred act between two people who love one another are related to the many examples we have seen of seemingly legitimate gurus or spiritual teachers, and pastors or priests who have been involved in sex scandals of various kinds.

The work of Abraham Maslow offers some insight into "peaks" that we can experience as we make our way along our own path of development. Maslow used the term "peak experiences" to refer to moments where a person rises above their normal mode of consciousness. During a peak experience a person experiences a heightened state of awareness where there is a sense of being connected with their surroundings. In a way, a peak experience takes you outside of yourself so that you can experience whatever you are experiencing as fully as possible. Athletes often refer to this type of experience as "being in the zone."

Maslow was also interested in the concept of motivation and how our motives are organized. He came to view human needs as having a hierarchical structure that is relevant to our discussion of cognitive development. Maslow's theoretical hierarchy of needs begins with our basic physiological needs. These are our primitive needs for survival such as air, water, and food. The next class of needs involves our safety and physical security needs. Here we are concerned with physical shelter and our relationship with the environment around us.

At the next level of Maslow's hierarchy, our needs have a more social aspect to them. This involves our need to be loved and have a sense of belonging to our family or group. Love and belongingness needs are for companionship, affection, and acceptance of others. After that are our esteem needs, these involve a sense of appreciation from others. We can be motivated by a need to be appreciated or esteemed for some quality that we possess. These qualities may include intellectual abilities, or whatever ability we may have to help the society we live in to function and prosper.

Finally, for Maslow, there is the need for self-actualization. This involves the motivation to push ourselves to be all that we can be...to explore the limits of our capabilities. Towards the end of his life, Maslow suggested that some self-actualizers will push on further towards a need for self-transcendence. These people strive for a transcendence of the self, and have a more universal, integrated, and holistic view of the world. They are motivated by goals outside of themselves and see all of life as having a sacred aspect to it. Keep Maslow's hierarchy of needs in mind as we explore this theory of the evolution of consciousness with its nine levels.

Archaic Consciousness

We all begin at square one, in diapers and drooling on ourselves. Archaic consciousness is primarily a physical level ruled by sensations and impulses that normally lasts into the second or third year of an infant's life. The influential developmental psychologist Jean Piaget, who spent nearly sixty years studying how children progress from one stage of thinking to another, calls this the sensorimotor stage. Infants are eventually able to differentiate themselves from their mothers and then learn to explore the physical world around them.

We can speculate that archaic consciousness was probably the average mode of consciousness of early Stone Age peoples. Our ancient ancestors would have lived primarily by sensation and instinct as they developed means to survive in their environment. Their primary concerns would have been with their physical needs and survival from day to day.

Magical Consciousness

Children between the ages of two to three and seven or eight experience a magical mental world of imaginary friends, fairies, and the like. This inner world "is a polytheistic Disneyland, full of angels, bogeymen, Santa Claus, and talking animals, and all of these are projections of aspects of the child's own psyche."(2) Piaget called this level the preoperational stage. Here we have the emergence of symbolic thought, with language being the most obvious form of this symbolism.

Piaget also observed that children at this stage have a tendency to have difficulty in recognizing another person's point of view. They tend to see the world as revolving around themselves, and also have a difficult time distinguishing appearances from reality. Piaget also noticed that children at this level of thinking often display animism. This is the tendency to attribute life and lifelike qualities to inanimate objects.

From a cultural perspective, magical consciousness was the general level of consciousness in the polytheistic, animistic, tribally-organized ancient world. (3) These tribal cultures viewed nature as being alive with spirit and often thought of natural phenomena such as the sun or the moon as gods. Thunder and lightning, or a natural disaster of some kind would be seen as resulting from the actions of the gods.

They conceived of magic ceremonies or rituals using magic words as a means of appeasing the gods and controlling nature. We find evidence of infanticide and other forms of human sacrifice to find favour with the gods and to benefit the tribe as a whole in some way. Psychologically speaking, these gods are projections into the environment of aspects of the tribal peoples' own inner psyches. (4)

There is also evidence of tremendous wisdom to be found in the worldviews of these ancient cultures. They seemed to have a real sense of the interconnectedness and sacredness of life. There is an awareness of a universal life force that gives life to everything in the material world. In China this life force is called *chi*, in India it is *prana*, and the ancient Mayans spoke of the ebb and flow of *k'ul*. We usually find a great love and respect for Mother Earth. Sadly, once mankind collectively reached the next two levels this wisdom would often be overlooked and discounted.

Mythic Consciousness

Mythic consciousness is the level of children from the age of seven or eight to adolescence. A child has the realization that the world does not revolve around them and they begin to understand the importance of specific cultural roles. They see the roles that teachers, doctors, or the police have in their lives and they understand there is a need to follow the rules. Of course the dominant authority figures in their lives are their parents, with the father often being the source of retribution for bad behaviour.

Children learn to conform to their parent's view of what constitutes good or bad behaviour. A child is conditioned to think and act in ways that are considered proper in their society. Naturally, their parent's religious beliefs, ethnic group, political views, etc., will often be seen as superior to others. A child's country of residence "or ethnic group or religion is typically seen as the greatest in the world, blessed by God beyond all others."(5)

For mythic consciousness to arise the child's mind (or ego) must develop "to the point where it becomes the lord and master of the child's inner world."(6) In a sense the ego becomes the god of the psyche and this ego, "which is archetypically male, is now projected into the sky and becomes the monotheistic, patriarchal Sky God."(7) Likewise, conceptions of a "Satan" figure of some kind represent the projection of the psyche's shadow side.

Along with a child's emerging mental abilities comes the ability to reason, and a reinterpretation of their previous magical ways of viewing their world. Religious myths and symbols are often viewed in more concrete, literal ways and therefore symbolic spiritual teachings such as virgin births or talking snakes can be seen as actual events.

At the cultural level, mythic consciousness has often been dominant in the world's religious traditions. Here we find an emphasis on moral accountability and consequences for one's actions. Laws or rules for proper behaviour become very important to the group. These rules are often specific and wide ranging, including dietary laws, how often to pray, in what direction to face while praying, and guidelines for priestly rituals.

Rewards and punishments for following the rules become a strong motivational factor for members of the group to adhere to the laws of authority figures. Punishment for bad behaviour can be very severe, including being put to death. Generally, this system of rewards and punishments is extended to an afterlife and here we find varied conceptions of heavens and hells.

Thankfully, human sacrifice becomes abolished, but unfortunately for animals it was often replaced by animal sacrifice. The sacrifice of animals becomes one of the priestly functions as an offering to the monotheistic God (having had projected onto their God human qualities like anger and jealousy). Some people believe this sacrificing of animals "represented the sacrificing (putting under the control of the mind or ego) of the lower animal-like parts of human consciousness, particularly aggression and sexuality, so that the tribes could live together in a more or less civilized fashion."(8)

This leads into another common result of mythic consciousness – the subjugation of women. With several of the laws of the group pertaining to proper sexual behaviour, and the punishments being so severe, men abuse their position of power to oppress women. Jim Marion sums it up nicely:

> "The essence of the shift from magical to mythic consciousness is the struggle of the mind (seen as 'male') to take control of the human psyche. So it was imperative that the mind (and therefore men, especially given the male's aggressive and sexually promiscuous instincts) not be tempted to regress to the old level. Women, representing the body, sexuality, and emotions like aggression, had to be kept under wraps." (9)

Of course this remains a problem to this day. Just one example would be the head-to-toe *burqas* that women are required to wear in a few Muslim areas still strongly influenced by mythic level thinking.

Despite its negative aspects monotheistic mythic consciousness was a step forward from magical consciousness for several reasons. First, there was a more explicit rendering of the insight that God is One. Secondly, the stress on ethical behaviour produced an understanding of being accountable for one's actions. And thirdly, tribes could unite (although often through violent means) and agree upon a shared mythology and set of rules that led to the formation of "ancient empires and, much later, today's nation states."(10)

This transformation also produced what we now think of as "world religions." For the purpose of this discussion we will focus on the so-called "western traditions" of Zoroastrianism, Judaism, Christianity, and Islam.

Zoroastrianism is a little known tradition that emerged among the Indo-Iranian peoples of present day Iran. This tradition dominated the religious thinking of the vast Iranian empire for more than a thousand years before the conversion of most Iranians to Islam in the seventh century. The prophet Zarathustra (1000? BCE), called Zoroaster by the Greeks, is traditionally associated with the formation of the beliefs of this tradition. There are relatively few Zoroastrians today, however; there is little doubt that Zoroastrian teachings had a significant influence on later Jewish, Christian, and Islamic theological formulations.

Zoroastrians worship the one God, known to them as Ahura Mazda (meaning "Wise Lord"). There is a strong emphasis on morality, with the essence of the religion being summed up in the motto: good thoughts, good words, and good deeds. There is a sense of there being both good and evil forces in the world and the need for a person to choose to do good.

At the time of death each soul is judged according to the nature of their thoughts, words, and deeds. Those souls judged to be good pass through the bridge to heaven while those found lacking find the bridge too narrow to cross and fall to a hellish place. There is also a belief in a final judgement of some kind where the world will be liberated from the influence of evil once and for all.

The tradition we now refer to as Judaism is generally considered to be the first monotheistic religion, beginning with the figure of Abraham (ca. 2000 BCE). According to popular belief with Moses (ca. 1200 BCE) came a long list of rules for living, the most famous of which being the Ten Commandments. The teaching known as the great commandment is also attributed to Moses: "Hear, O Israel: The Lord is our God, the Lord is one. You shall love the Lord your God with all your heart, and with all your soul, and with all your might" (Deuteronomy 6:4-5).

Mythic level thinking has a tendency to be ethnocentric. What applies to the in-group often does not apply to outsiders. The group can place great importance in a commandment like "Thou shalt not kill" (Exodus 20:13), while condoning a great deal of killing.

Shortly after the giving of the Ten Commandments the Hebrew Bible tells of a successful war against the people of Midian where all of the adult male Midianites had been killed. The author of Numbers has Moses giving the officers of the army further instructions to "kill every male among the little ones, and kill every woman who has known a man by sleeping with him. But all the young girls who have not known a man by sleeping with him, keep alive for yourselves" (31:17-18).

Christians who have been strongly influenced by mythic consciousness have also done much killing in the last 2000 years. At least since the time of Constantine and his use of Christianity as a means to consolidate power for the Roman Empire in the fourth century have people suffered at the hands of Christians in positions of power. We are all aware of the most obvious examples like inquisitions, the Crusades, or the treatment of native peoples.

This dark side of Christianity reveals another tendency of mythic level thinking – believing that one's own rules, beliefs, mythology, are superior to those of "others" and

75

that it is important for "others" to convert to the proper way of believing. This tendency has also been strong throughout the history of Islam.

These beliefs are linked with viewing one's "sacred writings" as being inerrant or "the word of God." The necessary result of this kind of wishful thinking (the product of a desire for certainty and absolutes) is that the teachings of others that are in any way different from the writings considered by the in-group to be the word of God must then be false and even dangerous.

This issue of mythic beliefs regarding holy books is related to the problem of translation and interpretation. Spiritual teachings and stories often use symbolic imagery and metaphor in trying to convey spiritual truths. Many a person has killed or been killed because of differing interpretations of a metaphor.

Joseph Campbell described mythology as "an organization of symbolic images and narratives, metaphorical of the possibilities of human experience and the fulfillment of a given culture at a given time."(11) Differences in translating and interpreting religious writings result not only because of issues regarding different languages and social circumstances, but also because of the differing levels of consciousness of the interpreters.

The problem of translation and interpretation is also relevant to personal experiences. Whatever a person experiences (even experiences of a mystical nature) will be shaped by that person's cultural background, belief system, personal history and so on. A person influenced by mythic level thinking may have a spiritual experience (peak experience) that they then interpret to fit into their current way of thinking. This serves to strengthen their mythic beliefs, and using the example of a mythic Christian, may jolt them into an even greater desire to convert the world to believe in "their Jesus."

Occasionally someone attached to mythic beliefs or their own particular religious doctrine has a profound peak experience that transforms their way of thinking. One of the NDErs that Dr. Raymond Moody interviewed was a man who had studied at a seminary and who looked down on anyone who was not a member of his denomination or did not subscribe to his theological beliefs. After his NDE he told Dr. Moody:

> "A lot of people I know are going to be surprised when they find out that the Lord isn't interested in theology. He seems to find some of it amusing, as a matter of fact, because he wasn't interested at all in anything about my denomination. He wanted to know what was in my heart, not my head."(12)

The experiences of the prophet Muhammad in the seventh century would lead to the development of a new religion. The word Islam has a twofold meaning, it speaks of both peace and surrender. A Muslim is a person who professes Islam and strives for the peace that comes from the surrendering of one's self to God. One can become a Muslim by repeating before two Muslim witnesses the *Shahadah* (profession of faith): "I bear witness that there is no god but God, and I bear witness that Muhammad is the messenger of God."

Generally speaking, a Muslim sees the Oneness of God as the primordial faith that all the true prophets and messengers of God have preached. Islam recognizes that there have been many prophets throughout history and across cultures. Five of these prophets are given special distinction: Noah, Abraham, Moses, Jesus, and Muhammad. Jesus is held in very high regard within the tradition, although Christians who have deified Jesus are viewed to have committed a grave error. For Muslims, to worship an idol or a human being is the greatest sin.

Muhammad is seen as the greatest and the last of the prophets. The revelation given to Muhammad is believed to be a call for humanity to return to its original, primordial belief and Islam considers itself the final call to God. Muhammad's actions and words are considered to have been divinely inspired and his life is seen as a model for humans to strive for until the Day of Judgement.

The only miracle attributed to Muhammad is the production of the Qur'an. For many Muslims the Qur'an is an immutable heavenly book – the word of God. Tradition holds that it was revealed to Muhammad over a period of 22 years (610-632). The Qur'an is considered true scripture only in the original Arabic, any translations into other languages are considered mere interpretations. It is said that no other language can do justice to the poetic and powerful qualities of a recitation of the Qur'an in Arabic.

In just a couple of generations the message of Islam transformed a region that had been dominated by tribal polytheism. The religion quickly spread throughout the entire Arabian peninsula and then into Syria, the Persian Empire, Egypt, Turkey, and Spain. During a time (ca.

800-1200) when much of Western Europe was in a period of decline, Islamic culture flourished in cities like Baghdad and Cairo. Muslims made significant contributions in areas such as medicine, astronomy, and mathematics, and were also very interested in Greek philosophy.

Rational Consciousness

Rational consciousness generally emerges during adolescence, and with modern educational methods it should be attained to some degree by the average adult in contemporary society. A person's ability to reason expands beyond the concrete mythic level to be able to accommodate more abstract ideas and universal principles. With the development of rational consciousness comes the potential for a greater understanding in areas such as philosophy, mathematics, and science.

If the transition from mythic to rational progresses in a healthy way a person will become "more tolerant, less judgmental, more compassionate, more inclusive, less fearful, less aggressive, and more universally loving."(13) However, this transition is often a difficult one and the teen years can be a time of rebellion. The influence of the ego is very strong at this level. If this natural evolution to more rational, independent thinking is suppressed by parents or other authority figures there can be destructive consequences.

If their progression towards higher levels of consciousness is obstructed in some way, "teenagers" may seek altered states of consciousness through sex, drugs, video games, or music. Of course, alcohol remains the most popular mind-altering drug. If their evolving spiritual needs are not being met some people may become more susceptible to joining a cult of some kind. In extreme cases, combined with other socioeconomic factors, there may even be the joining of gangs and partaking in criminal activity (a kind of regression back to negative aspects of lower levels of consciousness).

Culturally speaking, rational consciousness is the dominant consciousness of the present age. Humanity experienced the beginning of a monumental shift in consciousness in the period known as the "Axial Age" (800 BCE – 200CE). Greek philosophers like Pythagoras, Socrates, Plato, and Aristotle would have a tremendous impact on future philosophical thinking. In the East there were many seminal figures, including the Buddha in India and Confucius in China. And of course, Jesus arose in the Middle East to forever change the course of human history.

These great souls (teaching from the highest levels of consciousness) planted the seeds which would result in a widespread growth in consciousness from mythic to rational and beyond. Or perhaps it would be better to say their teachings watered seeds that were always there lying dormant in our fields of consciousness. Many people would come along who would work the soil, so to speak, and bring the rational level to a place of prominence in the modern world. The following brief (and Eurocentric) overview of this progression will highlight a few of the people who made significant contributions.

The thirteenth century would produce many influential thinkers. Thomas Aquinas spent much of his life trying to prove that Christian theology is a rational discipline. One of his principle sources in trying to make this argument was the philosophical teachings of Aristotle. Roger Bacon emerged during this time as an early supporter of the need for a natural science grounded in experimentation.

The period known as the Renaissance (14-16th centuries) which began in Italy would produce many influential people including the extraordinary Leonardo da Vinci (1452-1519). One of the factors that led to this period of flourishing intellectual and artistic activity was the study of the works of Greek/Hellenistic writers and Muslim philosophers. There were many important inventions during this time, in Italy and elsewhere. The invention of the printing press in the early sixteenth century was critical to the spread of rational and scientific ideas.

The use of the printing press by Protestant reformers was crucial for spreading the ideas and objections that would result in the Protestant Reformation. Less than ten years after Martin Luther officially began his opposition to Church practice in 1517 there were close to one million pamphlets in circulation that brought the topics of his challenge to a wide audience. Shortly thereafter the Bible was translated into different languages, including Luther's own German translation, and became accessible to the general public. In 1604, King James 1 of England began the process that would result in the production of the popular King James Version of the Bible.

Francis Bacon (1561-1626) was one of the first people to clearly see the connection between science and the improvement of the human condition. He realized that knowledge was power and that scientific knowledge and invention could be powerful tools for progress. In his *Novum Organum* he "sets out nothing less than a philosophy of science based on the axiom that 'the improvement of men's minds and the improvement of his lot are one and the same thing.'"(14)

The so-called "Enlightenment" of the seventeenth and eighteenth centuries produced many of the scientists, philosophers, and political figures who would use rational principles to transform the western world. Sir Isaac Newton (1642-1727) was a mathematical genius as well as a brilliant innovator when it came to experimentation. His work would inspire future generations of scientific thinkers and greatly advance what has come to be known as the Scientific Revolution. Newton was a religious man, although his beliefs were unorthodox for his day. He was interested in alchemy and rejected the traditional Christian doctrine of the Trinity.

There were many influential philosophical thinkers during this period including John Locke, David Hume, and Immanuel Kant. Kant is generally considered the most influential philosopher of the Enlightenment. He viewed philosophy as "the science of the relation of all knowledge to the essential ends of human reason."(15)

Late in this period Mary Wollstonecraft wrote "A Vindication of the Rights of Woman" (1792). This book is regarded as the seminal English-language feminist work. She argued that women are as naturally rational as men and should have equal opportunities in education, work, and politics.

The views of Enlightenment thinkers regarding religion are varied and fascinating. Some people were very critical of the dominant religious beliefs at the time and advocated a kind of atheistic rationalism. Many others began to question traditional Christian doctrines while refusing to give up belief in a creator God. Beliefs in a natural, rational view of religion began to emerge which is referred to as "Deism." Generally speaking, Deists accepted the moral teachings of the Bible while rejecting its claims of supernatural, miraculous events.

Deists were critical of literal interpretations of miracles or the story of the Garden of Eden and advocated allegorical interpretations of many Biblical stories. Any descriptions of God as being angry, jealous, or condoning violence were considered blasphemous. It was not uncommon for Deist writers to argue that the practice of extreme asceticism and self-torture, along with violent religious persecution were evidence of mental illness. Deism was never an organized movement and would essentially die out in the nineteenth century, but it influenced many important figures at the time and other religious formulations such as Unitarianism.

The founding fathers of the United States of America were products of the Enlightenment. George Washington was an early supporter of religious tolerance and the freedom of religion. There is little doubt that he was influenced by Deism and he is said to have had close ties with American Freemasonry. Benjamin Franklin was very open-minded when it came to religion and once identified himself as a Deist. We know from his letters that John Adams sometimes wondered if the world would be a better place if it was free of religion.

The genius who was Thomas Jefferson (1743-1826) was a Deist who later turned to Unitarianism. As a young man

Jefferson greatly admired Francis Bacon, Isaac Newton, and John Locke. He proposed innovative educational reforms and was a powerful advocate of the complete separation of church and state. Jefferson also wrote an account of the life and teachings of Jesus extracted from the Gospel stories where he excluded any references to the divinity of Jesus, the Trinity, or miracles. Now known as the "Jefferson Bible" this account was intended for family and friends, and was published after his death.

It could be argued that the production of the Declaration of Independence, by a five-person committee which picked Jefferson to do the writing, was a turning point in the establishment of rational consciousness. Despite its overlooking of slavery and women this document paved the way for beliefs in universal human rights and freedoms. It can also be said that the Age of Reason had begun "to triumph politically with the French and American Revolutions of the eighteenth century."(16)

These events coincided with Adam Smith's publication in 1776 of his famous work "The Wealth of Nations." Smith saw capitalism as the natural system for a free economy and his views had a significant impact on economics. England was prospering and its banking system was strong with British currency being secure, and banks began lending money to industry. James Watt had introduced the steam engine in 1770, and by 1785 steam engines were installed in cotton factories to increase production. By 1806, the power loom was introduced by Edmund Cartwright, revolutionizing the textile industry.

Britain would make large amounts of money in textiles and become dominant with its factory economy.

These events and inventions along with a host of others in the nineteenth century would establish the Industrial Revolution. Charles Darwin publishes "On the Origin of Species" in 1859 and scientific theories regarding evolution begin to attract attention. In the early part of the twentieth century Albert Einstein would revolutionize the field of physics with his general theory of relativity and other achievements.

The twentieth century would bring many medical breakthroughs and technological advancements which would improve living conditions around the world. Science gained in recognition and prestige and its relationship with religion began to suffer to an even greater degree. Faith in religious systems that continued to put forth mythic views also began to decline. Sceptical views about religion began to spread and increasing numbers of people began to refer to themselves as agnostics.

Discarding their mythic beliefs some people would "throw out the baby Jesus with the bath water" and lose all faith in God. For many of these people faith in religious views was replaced by faith in science to provide answers for our place in the world. For them the mythic God had died, as Nietzsche had declared back in 1882, and they could not see the God beyond mythic conceptions of God.

Other people reacted to the growing scepticism regarding mythic views by retreating into a kind of entrenchment in the mythic. Cries for a return to the "old-time religion" rang out and the need to embrace the fundamentals of traditional religious belief. Some of these "fundamentalists" would lash out at perceived threats to their belief system. A few considered evolution to be an evil teaching, while others would resort to violence when it came to later issues like abortion.

The twentieth century was a time of unthinkable violence. A conservative estimate of the number of people killed in those 100 years would be something like 100 million. Clearly one of the negative results of our technological advances is the development of more effective weapons, including weapons of mass destruction. The availability of these weapons to people who are for the most part (psychologically speaking) at the level of troubled teenagers has been very destructive.

Many people today are experiencing varying degrees of cognitive dissonance as a result of having one foot in mythic and one foot in rational ways of thinking. Today it is not uncommon for pastors or priests to go for psychological counselling. This cognitive dissonance is one of the contributing factors to the increasing numbers of people suffering from depression and other forms of mental illness. It is also one of the many factors that results in suicide bombers and other kinds of religious violence.

The violence of the twentieth century was not limited to people. The environment has also suffered a great deal. Scientific advancement coupled with limited, egocentric thinking has resulted in an ecological disaster. Rain forests have been cut down and toxic chemicals have been dumped into water systems. Pollution has resulted in acid rain and an ozone hole opening over the Earth. Automotive emissions and other greenhouse gases have contributed to the growing problem of climate change.

Despite all of its accomplishments and progress, rational level thinking has caused many problems. The ecosystem is out of balance and this is a result of the number of human beings who are out of balance, both psychologically and spiritually. Jim Marion writes:

> "And it is the tyranny of the rational male ego that is the culprit here, the cause of all this imbalance. The development of the separate individualized ego was a colossal achievement for human consciousness. But the ego has now become the principal obstacle to further human progress."(17)

It is crucial that the world collectively moves beyond rational consciousness as quickly as possible. We need a restoration of balance and for more people to be able to think globally. There is a need for harmony and for true equality when it comes to the masculine and feminine energies in this world. Balance and harmony are needed in our relationship with nature, in our relationships with other people and cultures, and within ourselves.

Vision-Logic Consciousness

Vision-logic consciousness is a rapidly emerging level where a person is able to think from many different perspectives. There is a genuine interest in people of different cultures, religions, and races. There is also growing concern for global issues in areas such as the environment, and an appreciation of pluralism and diversity. This is the level of consciousness "of many great artists, writers, international financiers, scientists, and philosophers."(18)

The emergence of the field of comparative religion is one early example of the growing interest in different cultures and religions. Max Muller emphasized how important it was to have knowledge of many religious traditions and often said, "He who knows one, knows none."(19) Muller was an important figure in translating and bringing attention to Hindu spiritual writings like the Rig Veda. Many scholars of comparative religion have made contributions to ecumenical pursuits, the growing acceptance of religious pluralism, and interfaith dialogue.

Modern theosophy emerged at the same time as the field of comparative religion to bring its own unique (and often controversial) contributions to the study of different cultures and religions. The official objectives of the Theosophical Society as stated in 1896 are as follows:

- To form a nucleus of the Universal Brotherhood of Humanity, without distinction of race, creed, sex, caste or colour.
- To encourage the study of comparative religion, philosophy and science.
- To investigate unexplained laws of Nature and the powers latent in man. (20)

One of the many interesting and unusual aspects of the Theosophical Society was the prominence of women in its leadership. After the death of its founder Helena Blavatsky, two other women named Alice Bailey and Annie Besant became influential leaders.

It could be argued that vision-logic consciousness began to emerge to a significant degree in the 1960s and

1970s. Beliefs in universal human rights and freedoms and that all people (not just white males) were created equal came to the forefront in a powerful way. The Women's Movement and its fight for cultural and political equality made significant strides in the 1960s.

The African-American Civil Rights Movement and its struggle for racial equality also made progress at this time. Martin Luther King Jr. delivered his "I Have a Dream" speech in 1963, and was awarded the Nobel Peace Prize in 1964. At the exact same time in South Africa, Nelson Mandela was jailed because of his opposition to apartheid.

This level produces the ability to move beyond egocentric and ethnocentric thinking towards what could be called a worldcentric or global perspective. The United Nations was an early product of this kind of thinking. This perspective gave birth to organizations like UNICEF, with its work for children around the world. In 1959 the UN General Assembly adopts the Declaration of the Rights of the Child. Shortly thereafter UNICEF expands its interests to include children's rights to protection, education, healthcare, shelter and good nutrition.

Technological advances in the twentieth century brought new means for people to travel around the world and new abilities to communicate on a global scale. This not only led to more interaction among people of different cultural backgrounds but also to people around the world learning from people of other cultures. For instance, here in the West there was a surge of popularity in traditionally eastern teachings like Buddhism, yoga, and t'ai chi. Increased communication between East and West has also contributed to more holistic and preventative approaches to medicine.

Perhaps the most obvious result of global thinking is increased concern for the welfare of the planet itself. Vision-logic is the consciousness of "the greens." The late 1960s and 1970s saw the rise of the modern green movement.

Environmental activism began to have an effect both on government policy and on people becoming more aware of ecological concerns. Here in Canada, David Suzuki has been a leader in this regard since the 1970s. He has worked to educate the public and to find ways for society to live in balance with the natural world. In recent years Al Gore has done a tremendous job of bringing attention to environmental issues like climate change.

This level may sound wonderful but it also has a shadow side. While the human personality has become more integrated and has a greater sense of freedom, this can be "a level of profound angst and inner unrest."(21) We saw this angst reflected in the writings of the existential philosophers of the early twentieth century. One aspect of existentialism was its critique of rationalism for its inability to provide meaning.

This shift in modern philosophical thought, which perhaps began with Nietzsche in the late nineteenth century, became most apparent in the 1960s and 1970s. In particular, several influential thinkers emerged out of the French structuralist movement at this time, including Jacques Derrida and Michel Foucault. These intellectuals had a significant impact on a new school of thought that would come to be known as poststructuralist and/or postmodern.

Postmodern thinking has provided many useful insights into how we view the world. Clearly there is a subjective aspect to whatever a person perceives as truth at any given time or place. It is important to understand context and the degree to which our perceived reality is the result of social construction. Everyone views the world through their own unique "interpretive lens." Most importantly what we see through our "interpretive lens" is filtered through whatever our level of consciousness may be at that moment.

However, postmodern thinking taken to its extreme results in relativism to an absurd degree, can come across as arrogant, and often approaches nihilism. Ken Wilber points out that there is a hypocritical quality to the views of extreme postmodernists:

> "They claimed it was universally true that there are no universal truths, that it is a cultural invariant that there are no cultural invariants, that it is objectively true that there is no objective truth. They claimed, in short, that their position was superior in a world where nothing was supposed to be superior."(22)

A person at the vision-logic level for the most part continues to identify their "self" with the mind. The ego continues to have a significant influence. Some people will take great pride in their superior knowledge compared to modern and pre-modern peoples, their environmentalism, or their inclusive and tolerant beliefs. Their feelings towards people they perceive to have outdated beliefs concerning religion can be anything but loving and compassionate.

Having left behind mythic religious views back at the rational level many people at this stage have a void in their lives when it comes to spirituality. Even individuals who seem to have it all when it comes to worldly success can struggle to find meaning and are often dealing with a great deal of inner turmoil. There also seems to be a tendency for people at this level these days to have issues with fear.

For people with little or no spiritual beliefs there is often an underlying fear of death, whether conscious or unconscious. These days this fear seems to be reflected in obsessive views regarding the physical body and desires to live as long as possible. Fuelled by the media we are seeing increased levels of fear in many areas including: fear of cancer, fear of high cholesterol, fear of global warming, and fear of terrorists. Being aware of these things and what contributes to them is a good thing, living our lives in fear is unhealthy.

Unfortunately many people deal with this inner turmoil, fear, and the stress of living in this fast-paced postmodern world by turning to alcohol or other drugs. It is no coincidence that the 1960s and 1970s also saw the rise of the drug culture. There is a need for more and more people to embrace a balanced, healthy and spiritual lifestyle.

Vision-logic will have become the dominant consciousness when we see a greater focus on the need for education about the world's diverse religious traditions. We will see more progress in the area of human rights and equality, particularly in regards to women, minorities, and a person's sexual orientation. There will be significant changes in how we do business on a global scale so that there is a much less harmful impact on the environment. And finally, we will see increasing numbers of people who view all of creation as having spiritual significance and who "deeply appreciate and value their own interior lives."(23)

Psychic Consciousness

A person with psychic consciousness no longer identifies their self with the rational mind, instead they begin to identify with that part of themselves that observes body, emotions, and mind. People at this level are usually spiritual seekers who have learned to go within themselves in their search for meaning and personal growth. Meditation often becomes a focus of their spiritual practice and intuitive/psychic abilities usually become enhanced. This is the level of consciousness of many poets, shamans, prophets, and clairvoyants.

We are all psychic to varying degrees, in a similar way to how everyone has some amount of musical ability. As spiritual beings we all have the potential to experience extrasensory perception. Intuitive skills can be developed through spiritual practices but some people have more natural gifts then others. There are people who display psychic abilities at a young age. Why do some people have more intuitive abilities then others? How do you explain a musical prodigy like Mozart? For many people a significant aspect of the answers to these questions comes from an understanding of karma and reincarnation.

There are many examples of Hindu and Buddhist writings that advise their readers to be aware (and wary) of the development of psychic powers with spiritual practice. These abilities have been spoken of across cultures for all of recorded history. There are the medicine men of native traditions, the oracles of Delphi in the Greek tradition, and the prophets of Israel. In China there is a long history of divination and beliefs that certain individuals possess special powers.

The Jesus that is presented in the Gospels is very psychic. He is described as being able to read people's minds (Mark 2:8, Luke 5:22) and there are the references to his healing abilities and other miraculous events. The authors of the Gospels also wanted it understood that Jesus had the gift of prophecy. For instance they have him predicting the destruction of the temple in Jerusalem and his own death. It is recorded that Jesus said that we have the same psychic potential: "the one who believes in me will also do the works that I do and, in fact, will do greater works than these, because I am going to the Father" (John 14:12).

Judging from Paul's letters he believed that many early Christians had developed psychic abilities. He describes these abilities as gifts of the spirit. Paul taught that some people would develop the gift of healing, others would be able to work miracles, and a few would have the gift of prophecy and other abilities (1Corinthians 12:1-11).

In medieval times to possess (or perhaps more accurately to be accused of possessing) these kinds of powers could be very dangerous, particularly if you were a woman. For example, we now have a good understanding of how "witches" were used as scapegoats for societal problems. The nineteenth century saw a rise in interest in what has been called spiritualism. Today in our sophisticated postmodern world there is no shortage of people who claim to be psychics, mediums, spiritual healers and the like.

There are dangers to be aware of when it comes to this level of consciousness. One of these is obvious, and that is charlatans claiming to have spiritual gifts for the purpose of making money and/or gaining notoriety. Discernment is needed whether we are talking about psychic hotlines or a preacher in an established church. It is also unwise to fool around with things like Ouija boards or to experiment with drugs in the hopes of inducing a spiritual experience.

A less obvious danger often associated with this level is the problem of spiritual pride. In his first letter to the Corinthians it seems clear that Paul is concerned that some of his followers there have become proud of their psychic abilities. He advises them to not get sidetracked and forget about more important spiritual attributes like humility, patience, and especially the ability to love. This advice is found in some of the most famous passages in the New Testament:

> "If I speak in the tongues of mortals and of angels, but do not have love, I am a noisy gong or a clanging cymbal. And if I have prophetic powers, and understand all mysteries and all knowledge, and if I have all faith, so as to remove mountains, but do not have love, I am nothing...Love is patient; love is kind; love is not envious or boastful or arrogant or rude... It bears all things, believes all things, hopes all things, endures all things... For we know only in part, and we prophesy only in part; but when the complete comes, the partial will come to an

end. When I was a child, I spoke like a child, I thought like a child, I reasoned like a child; when I became an adult, I put an end to childish ways. For now we see through a glass, darkly, but then we will see face to face. Now I know only in part; then I will know fully, even as I have been fully known. And now faith, hope, and love abide, these three; and the greatest of these is love" (13:1-2, 4, 7, 9-13).

Spiritual pride is an issue in all religious traditions as well as less traditional forms of spirituality. In particular it is a common problem in "new age" spirituality. Many "new age" type teachings place great emphasis on the "Self" and often equate it with God...this is a mistake. Our true self is not perfect...we are NOT God. It is true that we all have a spark of divinity at the very core of our being as children of God, but compared to God we are but a speck of dust.

It seems to me that a significant amount of this false information about our true self comes from channelers who are attempting to allow a supposedly higher dimensional being to communicate through them. This is a dangerous practice that should always be avoided. Some of the information that comes through sounds very clever but it is not trustworthy.

The ego still has an influence at the level of psychic consciousness and will now try to define itself as more spiritual and holy than others. Jesus emphasized the importance of humility and taught: "All who exalt themselves will be humbled, and all who humble themselves will be exalted" (Matthew 23:12).

Many of us have little psychic ability and that is perfectly fine, in some respects it is a blessing. This level of consciousness is much more about an inner growth in awareness than developing psychic skills. To know God we must turn within; through prayer, meditation, and striving to let that mind be in us which was in Christ Jesus. Increased levels of awareness allow us to see new levels of meaning in inspired writing like the Pauline teaching that there is "one God and Father of all, who is above all and through all and in all" (Ephesians 4:6).

This level brings increased awareness of the influence of our thoughts, emotions, words and actions on our spiritual and physical well-being. We begin to understand that the Spirit of God is a vibrant force of cosmic energy that moves through us and gives us life. The gifted medical intuitive Dr. Caroline Myss teaches that:

> "Because Divine energy is inherent in our biological system, every thought that crosses our minds, every belief we nurture, every memory to which we cling translates into a positive or negative command to our bodies and spirits."(24)

This understanding reminds us of the importance of mindfulness and should bring gratitude along with a more intense love of God. We realize that every moment of every day is a precious opportunity to express our love for God through our thoughts, words, and deeds. Life takes on a whole new meaning and we begin to tap into our full potential.

Subtle Consciousness

At the subtle level the ego begins to fade away and there are often illuminating insights into the nature of reality. This stage often culminates with what the Christian mystics call "the dark night of the soul." The dark night is a difficult period which ends with the dissolution of the ego and a person being reborn in spirit.

This level usually involves mind expanding experiences and is often a time of great creativity and discovery. For a person with considerable psychic abilities there may be visions or revelations and other extraordinary phenomena. In the Catholic mystic tradition subtle consciousness is referred to as the illuminative way, or the way of infused contemplation.

What we may or may not experience at this stage will depend on our own unique situation including our intellectual abilities and our belief system. As usual Jim Marion sums it up beautifully:

> "Each person's experience will be different because, by the time the soul grows into the subtle level, it has become greatly individuated, having integrated all the experiences of many lifetimes, often liberating those experiences from the depths of the unconscious. The wisdom gained in these experiences is collected and kept. The pain and suffering of all those experiences are gradually released, thus purifying the soul and the body to go to higher vibrational levels."(25)

The person at this stage will be open to new ways of thinking and viewing the world around them. They will have a more flexible, detached system of beliefs and be much less restricted by preconceived assumptions and concepts. This new way of being will have some kind of a "spiritual" aspect to it probably involving a reverence for the "mind of God," but will also have a more down-to-earth quality probably including a reverence for nature.

I do not like to speculate about the level of consciousness of historical figures but in the case of Albert Einstein I will make an exception. There is no doubt in my mind that this extraordinary genius was an old soul who was operating in the subtle realms for most of his adult life. Einstein not only gave us ground breaking insights into the ways of nature, he was also wise in his understanding of human nature. Besides his contributions to science he was an advocate for human rights, social justice, and world peace.

Einstein did not believe in a personal God and was not affiliated with any religious organizations, but he did consider himself a religious person. Once at a dinner party he was questioned if it was true that he described himself as religious and he replied:

> "Yes, you can call it that. Try and penetrate with our limited means the secrets of nature and you will find that, behind all the discernible concatenations, there remains something subtle, intangible and inexplicable. Veneration for this force beyond anything we can comprehend is my religion. To that extent I am, in point of fact, religious."(26)

God for this type of belief system is in an impersonal cosmic order driven by the laws of cause and effect. Einstein said that he believed in the God of Spinoza. He was a great admirer of Baruch Spinoza, a seventeenth century Jewish philosopher. Spinoza had rejected the traditional (mythic) conception of God and is now considered one of the more influential contributors to the Enlightenment.

Einstein received instruction regarding his Jewish tradition at home while attending a Catholic public primary school. This early religious instruction with its Jewish and Catholic elements seems to have contributed to his later respect for wise religious teachings from various traditions. The depth of his understanding is reflected in his well known quote: "Few are those who see with their own eyes and feel with their own hearts."

Einstein's unorthodox religious views allowed him to regard the relationship of science and religion as complementary and even dependent on one another. Thus we have his famous dictum: "Science without religion is lame, religion without science is blind."

Once while being interviewed by two Irish intellectuals, Einstein declared, "I am of the opinion that all the finer speculations in the realm of science spring from a deep religious feeling, and that without such feeling they would not be fruitful."(27) Einstein knew the joy of receiving illuminating insights and he seems to have sensed they came from a place beyond the norm of human understanding. Despite all of his accomplishments and acclaim his deep understanding kept him in awe of nature and instilled in him a humble quality.

A profound humility is required before a person can move on to higher levels of consciousness. As we begin the gradual ascent to the next level (the causal), "we also begin a simultaneous descent into a spiritual crisis the like of which we have never before experienced."(28) St. John of the Cross, a sixteenth century Catholic mystic and poet, called this descent the dark night of the soul.

We must be purged of the darkness within us; our fears, selfish desires, and pride so that we can be filled with light. The bride (the soul) must be pure before the alchemical marriage to the bridegroom (the Christ) can take place. The self must be emptied so that all that remains is the true self. This was one of the central Pauline teachings for the spiritually mature, as we find in the letter to the Ephesians:

> "You were taught to put away your former way of life, your old self, corrupt and deluded by its lusts, and to be renewed in the spirit of your minds, and to clothe yourselves with the new self, created according to the likeness of God in true righteousness and holiness" (4:22-24).

The story of Jesus spending forty days in the wilderness and being tempted by the devil is symbolic of the dark night of the soul. This difficult period ends when a person faces down their inner demons and prevails. Then they are prepared for the death (or crucifixion) of the ego and a rebirth (or resurrection) into a whole new way of being.

One of the symbolic meanings of Jesus on the cross and his death and resurrection is this process of inner transformation that we all must experience. No one can see the kingdom of God without this experience of being born anew (John 3:3).

Causal Consciousness

Having been reborn in spirit a person becomes psychologically whole, free of projecting their best and worst qualities onto others. At this level a person identifies with their true self and is more and more free of conditioned thinking. Their heart is open and they feel the Love of God working on and through them on deeper and deeper levels.

For the Christian tradition this means that a person has put on the mind of Christ, and this level would properly be called Christ consciousness. From a Buddhist perspective it could be said that a person has awoken to their true Buddha nature, and this level could be called Buddha consciousness or Buddha mind. For the Hindu it might be referred to as Krishna consciousness, although Paramahansa Yogananda taught that in Hindu scripture it is called *Kutastha Chaitanya*.

Having endured the dark night we will have learned true humility and a level of trust and faith in God beyond anything we have experienced before. Our doubts and fears will have faded away and we experience a gradual unfolding of love for everyone. It is as the Johannine community believed:

"God is love, and those who abide in love abide in God, and God abides in them. Love has been perfected among us in this: that we may have boldness on the day of judgement, because as he is, so are we in this world. There is no fear in love, but perfect love casts out fear; for fear has to do with punishment, and whoever fears has not reached perfection in love" (1John 4:16-18).

Jim Marion describes this stage as "the level of true Christian love, which is spiritual love identical to what the Buddhist masters call true compassion."(29) Christ consciousness is the way to the Kingdom of God. No one comes to the Father except through the Son (John 14:6).

Nondual Consciousness

This is the kingdom of God. This is the level from which Jesus spoke when he said, "The Father and I are one" (John 10:30), and that he hoped we would all reach when he prayed to the Father "that they may be one, as we are one" (John 17:22). This is "the place in consciousness he told us to strive for in which we are perfect as the Father is perfect" (Matt. 5:48). (30)

The relatively few who have reached this level tell the rest of us that it is beyond words, and that it is finally possible to live fully in the present moment. The illusion of this field of opposites melts away and "all the polar opposites disappear for they are now all seen as complements that forever make wholes."(31) They have reached that place in consciousness where "the devil, or duality, is now finally and completely vanquished."(32) The two have become one.

The Circle of Life

You would be correct in observing that this path of development sounds like a long and difficult journey. There is no doubt that the evolutionary process can be brutal and painful. Jesus made it clear that it is not easy to enter into the kingdom of God. The famous teaching of how rare it is for a rich person to enter the kingdom is just one example. No accomplishments in this world that are worthwhile are easy or automatic, and there is no exception when it comes to the salvation of our souls.

Many people today would like to believe they are saved by simply believing in a particular religious system or teaching. In some cases the incredibly important and difficult inner transformation where we are "born anew" has been reduced to the recitation of a prescribed "mantra" of some kind.

Belief can be an important step, akin to starting a car, but there remains a considerable distance to travel before reaching our destination. Belief leads to faith, faith leads to experience, and experience leads to God.

Again, it is important to note that this theory of consciousness development that we have just discussed is not a smooth linear process. There is an ongoing struggle between transcendence and repression at each stage of human evolution. (33) Each successive level both transcends and includes the previous level. Ken Wilber writes that as "the higher stages of consciousness emerge and develop, they themselves include the basic components of the earlier worldview, then add their own new and more differentiated perceptions."(34)

Until we collectively reach the causal level (and we are a long way from that) each new way of viewing the world will bring new advancements as well as new problems. The twentieth century demonstrated this in dramatic ways. The rational and vision-logic levels may be farther along in the developmental process than magical or mythic but they are far away from the Kingdom.

Every soul that comes into this world is doing something that is courageous and heroic. Life in this world involves a great deal of pain and suffering. We make progress through a series of births, deaths, and rebirths as we travel along the path of human evolution. Why does it have to be so difficult and painful? Joseph Campbell spoke to this question in his discussion with Bill Moyers in this way: "That is just the way it is, but by God you are alive and it is spectacular!"

The good news is that we do not need to understand quantum physics or postmodern philosophy to progress to the highest stages. It is also unnecessary to pay gurus or religious organizations for the means to reach higher levels. One of the great blessings of this postmodern age is the access we have to helpful information regarding our health and well-being, including our spiritual well-being. God may seem to be an elusive prey in this world, hiding behind and within physical form, but with enough diligence and determination spiritual hunters will find what they are looking for.

Part 3

The Function of Religion

If there is righteousness in the heart, there
will be beauty in the character.
If there is beauty in the character, there
will be harmony in the home.
If there be harmony in the home, there
will be order in the nation.
If there be order in the nation, there
will be peace in the world.

--- Confucius

The word "religion" is derived from the Latin *religio,* which refers to binding or reconnecting. Religion is meant to awaken us to our connection with the Source of life and to facilitate the awakening of our true self. By connecting to that which is real or true, we transcend that which is unreal or false. By overcoming our false/egoic self we are bound to our true self.

Our true self (or spirit) resides in the center of our spiritual heart. And we all have a direct connection to the Source of Love through our inner heart. All religions should place great emphasis on reminding their adherents of the importance of the quality and condition of their spiritual hearts.

The religions of this world have served many functions in their respective cultures. Religion has had a close relationship with the social and political developments in almost any given society. This section is about the potential for religion to help produce spiritual transformations within people which then lead to psychological/spiritual development and cultural change.

Before getting into religious teachings that can have transformative effects I would like to discuss three of the most important functions of religion. The first of these functions "is to awaken and maintain in the person an experience of awe, humility, and respect in recognition of that ultimate mystery that transcends every name and form."(1) Mythological stories can help invoke in us a sense of wonder and a reverence for the Source of life.

The story of the Garden of Eden with the tree of life and the tree of the knowledge of good and evil is one example. Having eaten from the tree of the knowledge of good and evil we find ourselves in the field of duality and having been "cast out" of the world of nonduality. Finding our way back to the Garden and the tree of life has been a long and challenging journey. Religious traditions should provide "a map" and point out potential obstacles as we travel along the spiritual path.

In the Christian tradition there is the mystery surrounding the life, death, and resurrection of Jesus. We find teachings on the mystery of the kingdom of God and the mystery of Christ. There are rituals like the Eucharist that help to keep us connected with Christ and remind us of the need for Christ to live in and through us. Beautiful cathedrals with their stained glass windows can transport us to another place psychologically and fill us with a sense of awe and wonder.

A second function of religion is to aid us in purifying and transforming our minds. Religious instruction should help people to raise their level of awareness...to accelerate growth in their consciousness...to guide people towards the highest level of consciousness possible for a human being. That level of love and unity from which Jesus preached, and prayed that we would all reach also.

Please understand that this nondual level of consciousness is not reached by developing our minds and becoming very intelligent. It is found and realized deep within us at the very core of our true self after letting God's Love help to transform our minds and free our hearts, and it is about becoming very loving and compassionate. It is only when we are able to "get out of our heads" that we can truly live from the heart. Then we are better able to connect with the "God within" and live a life filled with joy, gratitude, and inspiration.

And naturally, the third function of religion is to help open and purify the hearts of people to love and compassion for others. "Create in me a clean heart, O God, and put a new and steadfast spirit within me" prayed the author of Psalm 51. For a Christian the life and death of Jesus was the turning point for this restoring of our hearts and spirits to take place.

The prophet Jeremiah foresaw a time when the Lord would make a new covenant: "I will put my law within them, and I will write it on their hearts" (31:33). In his letters to the early Christian communities Paul understood that the new covenant would be for all peoples and that while physical circumcision was a seal of the old covenant, the seal of the new covenant would be "a spiritual circumcision" (Colossians 2:11). In his letter to the Romans he states clearly that "real circumcision is a matter of the heart - it is spiritual and not literal" (2:28-29).

Spiritually speaking we are all brothers and sisters. In the Buddhist tradition it is believed that we all have an innate ability to develop and express true love and compassion towards all sentient beings. This ability can be cultivated to extend beyond our immediate loved ones towards unconditional love and compassion for all. It is taught that love and compassion are the source of qualities like tolerance, kindness and forgiveness. There is also an understanding that it is from the development of these qualities that a person finds inner peace and true happiness.

Religious teachings should help enable us to make progress towards the kingdom of God. One of the most comprehensive teachings that will lead to an acceleration of growth (if practised consistently, and especially if it is combined with a love for God and a longing to be closer to God) is The Eightfold Path of the Buddha.

The first two aspects of The Eightfold Path have to do with the cultivation of wisdom; they are Right Understanding and Right Thought. The next three are concerned with morality and are Right Speech, Right Action, and Right Livelihood. The final three aspects are about developing concentration and the determination it takes to make progress on the spiritual path. These are Right Effort, Right Mindfulness, and Right Meditation.

Right Understanding

Right Understanding begins with a solid understanding of the Four Noble Truths. Knowledge of our habitual thinking and behaviours that contribute to suffering and dissatisfaction is a key to positive change. It is also important to understand the distinction between knowledge and wisdom.

In this postmodern information age we have access to a tremendous amount of information. It is not the knowledge that comes from being informed that is so important, but the wisdom used in the application of that knowledge. Dr. Roger Walsh in his wonderful book "Essential Spirituality" sums it up in this way: "Knowledge informs us, wisdom transforms us."(2)

One important ingredient in developing wisdom is self-knowledge. It is wise to have a clear understanding of our strengths and weaknesses. In addition to this knowledge it is critical to understand the role the ego plays in feeding us with thoughts and feelings of superiority and inferiority.

That which we refer to as "the ego" does not really exist. Our cumulative development of a separate sense of "self" plays a significant role in our progress but then must ultimately be overcome for us to reach our destination. This egoic self is a psychological construct sustained by the energy of thoughts and emotions that arise out of fear. Cultural conditioning contributes to these fears and they produce selfishness, greed, hate and the like.

Simply by being aware of our fears, selfish desires, cravings and attachments they begin to lose their power. Awareness of our bad habits and habitual patterns of negative thinking helps us to make progress in overcoming them. It is important to focus on the positive and understand the impact of our thoughts and emotions so that we do not put our energy into negative tendencies. Some of these bad habits and patterns of negativity have deep roots. For this reason it is important to have an understanding of karma.

Karma is the energy we use – in action, the reaping of what we have sown, the physical consequences of the choices we make. Sayings like "He who lives by the sword shall die by the sword" (Matthew 26:52) and "what goes around comes around" are echoing this spiritual principle. The law of karma (or cause and effect) is an impersonal law. It is as Jim Marion writes:

"We inherit karma on the physical level (our genes), the emotional/psychic level (the habits we carry over from past lives), the soul level

112

(the level of consciousness we realized in past lives), and the cultural level (the family, society, religion, economic status we are born into). That is our inheritance. It can be positive, negative, or neutral."(3)

Belief in the Christ within and our true Buddha nature are keys to overcoming our karmic inheritance. As children of God we all have the same potential and we should rejoice in the words of Jesus: "Do not be afraid, little flock, for it is your Father's good pleasure to give you the kingdom" (Luke 12:32).

Right Thought

Our thoughts have power and it is important to be mindful of our thought patterns. The Buddhist tradition probably places more emphasis on the power of the mind than any other. The opening lines of "The Dhammapada" teach us that:

> "What we are today comes from our thoughts of yesterday, and our present thoughts build our life of tomorrow: our life is the creation of our mind."

Buddhism teaches that we are all interconnected and interdependent. Therefore our thoughts and intentions towards life in general, ourselves, and others not only have the power to shape our perception of reality but also to influence what life brings our way. Unfortunately many people's perception of reality is badly distorted by selfish, fearful, egoic thinking.

Much of our fear and anxiety is produced by this distorted way of thinking. A great deal of this kind of thinking is nothing but fantasy; what we imagine people will think about us or fearful thinking about the future. As Dr. Roger Walsh puts it: "We do not usually fear reality, what is actually happening, but rather our own thoughts and fantasies about what may happen."(4) An important tool for reducing these fears and anxieties is striving to live in the present moment and understanding that the future only exists in our imagination.

Any thoughts of the future should utilize positive imaging. One of the best times to feed our minds positive affirmations and images is prior to sleeping in that in-between state of being asleep or awake. I like to begin by thinking about having a good night's sleep and with thoughts like, "I will feel revitalized in the morning," and "I am healthy and strong." Then I visualize my body being healthier and stronger. If there are other areas in your life that you would like to improve then see yourself being successful in those pursuits and goals.

It is possible to train the mind and to rise above unhealthy thinking. In the words of Paul we should strive to "take every thought captive to obey Christ" (2Corinthians 10:5). Clearly one important aspect of cultivating healthy states of mind is bringing constant attention to what we feed our minds. Our mental health will be influenced by the quality of our interactions and conversations with other people, the television shows or the movies we watch, the music we listen to, or the books we read.

Beyond striving to eliminate unhealthy products from our mental diet there is the need to be aware of our thoughts and emotions that arise in response to whatever situation or activity we find ourselves participating in. The conscious use of positive thinking and positive affirmations can be helpful in breaking old patterns of reacting to stimuli that are detrimental to spiritual growth and peace of mind.

It is wise to have some mind-training slogans that resonate with us to counter negative tendencies. For instance when egotistical thoughts arise they could be met with the thought "all praise and glory be to God." Another example would be a person who finds themselves in a situation that provokes feelings of anxiety and fearful thinking telling themselves that "I can do all things through Christ which strengthens me" (Philippians 4:13).

In this turbulent world of multitasking and text messaging it is beneficial to take some mental breaks. One example of a break of this kind would be closing your eyes for a few moments, taking some deep breaths, and feeding your mind a saying like "Peace, be still" (Mark 4:39).

Religious teachings should be constantly evolving and adapting to an ever-changing world. The insights from modern psychology have provided us with some new ways of understanding how our minds work. Everyone should have a good understanding of ego defence mechanisms like repression, projection, and rationalization.

Right Speech

We human beings have an amazing ability to rationalize unacceptable behaviour. A significant amount of our verbal communication is influenced by this kind of rationalization in the service of the ego. Putting people down behind their backs, gossip, foul or abusive language, and dishonest/deceitful words all reflect our lower nature. Buddhist tradition holds that the Buddha placed great emphasis on the need for Right Speech.

When our words are more reflective of our Buddha nature they are "articulated without guile, masked ego needs, conflict, or hidden agendas."(5) Just as with our thoughts we need to bring constant attention to what comes out of our mouths. Negative patterns of speech like the excessive use of profanity become a habit. Self-discipline and determination along with the practice of mindfulness of our words and tendencies will eventually break down any harmful habitual patterns of speech.

The Gospel of Matthew has Jesus speaking powerfully about the need for Right Speech:

> "I tell you, on the day of judgment you will have to give an account for every careless word you utter; for by your words you will be justified, and by your words you will be condemned" (12:36-37).

> "Listen and understand: it is not what goes into the mouth that defiles a person, but it

is what comes out of the mouth that defiles"
(15:10-11).

One of the classics of Christian literature "The Imitation of Christ" has been a source of wisdom for over 500 years. Its author had little use for mindless chatter and gossip. His advice is to not be preoccupied with the lives of other people and that,

> "When it is right and proper to speak, speak to edify. Evil habits and neglect of spiritual progress are the main cause of our failure to guard the tongue...We could enjoy much peace if we did not busy ourselves with what other people say and do, for this is no concern of ours."(6)

There is an old Arabic proverb that says "open your mouth only if what you are going to say is more beautiful than silence." I love to have regular periods of silence and solitude. I also love these words of Father Thomas Keating: "Silence is the language God speaks and everything else is a bad translation."(7) The most obvious benefit of periods of silence and solitude is they aid our ability to make progress in stilling and purifying our minds.

Right Action

Through the conscientious practice of Right Action we cultivate goodness and virtue within ourselves and help to transform the world around us. The old saying "our actions speak louder than words" is very true. There is a teaching attributed to the Buddha which states very simply and clearly the importance of goodness in action:

> "Do not do anything harmful; do only what is good; purify and train your own mind: This is the teaching of the Buddha; this is the path to enlightenment."(8)

Buddhist teachers advocate nonviolence and the need to develop a reverence for life. Thich Nhat Hanh has been a champion of peace and nonviolence for decades and teaches that it is not enough to vow not to kill. In whatever ways we can, we should work to spread the teaching of nonviolence and help to prevent others from engaging in destructive behaviour.

Taking from others that which is not freely given, in whatever form it takes, contributes to the suffering and lack of harmony in this world. Stealing has many forms. Modern spiritual teachers understand that the ancient teaching "do not steal" should be applied to areas like social injustice, unethical business practices, and the exploitation of the environment.

Buddhism teaches that increased awareness of the consequences of our actions will lead to progress in cultivating loving-kindness and compassion. Increased levels of loving-kindness and compassion produce a greater inclination to give of ourselves to others. Buddhist teachings stress the importance of generosity, and the positive impact of helping to alleviate the suffering in other people's lives.

It is not necessary for these good deeds and this generous giving to be on a large scale involving significant amounts of time and money. In his excellent book "Awakening the Buddha Within" the Buddhist teacher Lama Surya Das writes:

> "Call your local blood bank to give much-needed blood or platelets; become a volunteer for an organization that delivers food and other services to shut-ins; visit retirement homes or places that care for sick children without families; try to find homes for stray animals; sign up for an organization that provides emotional support or teaches reading skills to needy children. Recycle, recycle, recycle. Many cities, for example, have people who will recondition old bicycles to give to children who can't afford them. Donate your used computers, clothes, books, and tapes, as well as your services and money, to worthwhile charities. Try to look into the eyes and heart of each person you meet; try to treat everyone with kindness, warmth, and acceptance. Maybe you can't save the whole world all at once, but if you can make even one other person's life a little happier, you are making a difference. One pair of warm gloves for one pair of cold hands can help. One less piece of litter along the highway helps. Every smile helps."(9)

In my opinion another aspect of Right Action is striving to maintain a healthy lifestyle. Body, mind, soul, and spirit are all connected and our health and fitness levels will have an impact on our overall development. Again, one of the wonderful benefits to living in this information age is the access we now have to good information on nutrition and training methods.

It is important to keep hydrated by drinking plenty of water and healthy juices. Taking regular walks in nature is perhaps the most beneficial form of exercise. A daily stretching routine and/or yoga practice improves our flexibility and greatly benefits our ability to reach higher fitness levels while avoiding injuries. Strength training and cardio exercises build muscle and endurance. It is also important to alternate and change our workout routines in order to stimulate growth and avoid falling into the same routine where we plateau and stop reaching new heights of fitness.

Obviously the fuel we feed our bodies is very important. Fruits and vegetables should be the staples of any diet. We now know that it is best to eat small meals every few hours and to begin the day with a healthy breakfast. High levels of health and fitness produce increased levels of energy and improved mental functioning which then greatly benefit our spiritual pursuits.

The Buddha specifically taught that we are not to use intoxicants. The importance of mental clarity for spiritual practice would have originally been the foremost reason for this teaching. Today we have a good understanding of the harmful effects of alcohol and other drugs on both our mental and physical health.

We are now aware of the negative impact the use of alcohol has on virtually all of our internal organs, particularly those related to the digestive system. The use and abuse of alcohol has contributed to so much pain and suffering in this world. That this dangerous mind-altering drug continues to find social acceptability is truly sad. Hopefully attitudes towards alcohol will change in the near future in a similar way as they have recently in regards to smoking.

Of course one of the great dangers of using alcohol to self-medicate is that its intoxicating effects can lead to other harmful actions. How often is alcohol a factor in things like fighting, domestic violence, car accidents, or unwholesome sexual conduct? For those who would continue to rationalize the use of intoxicants I ask with Paul: "Do you not know that you are God's temple and that God's Spirit dwells in you?"(1 Corinthians 3:16).

The Christian tradition also preaches the importance of Right Action. The letter of James is particularly forceful in its reminder of the need for good works. We read that "a person is justified by works and not by faith alone...For just as the body without the spirit is dead, so faith without works is also dead" (James 2:24,26). Then there are the beautiful words attributed to Jesus:

> "You are the light of the world. A city built on a hill cannot be hid. No one after lighting a lamp puts it under the bushel basket, but on the lampstand, and it gives light to all in the house. In the same way, let your light shine before others, so that they may see your good works and give glory to your Father in heaven" (Matthew 5:14-16).

The teaching that provides the best foundation for Right Action can be found in one form or another in every wisdom tradition and is commonly known as the Golden

Rule. Confucius was one of the greatest teachers of ethical living this world has ever seen. He taught a version of the Golden Rule more than 500 years before the birth of Jesus and considered it one of his core teachings.

Jewish teachers have long understood the importance of this great spiritual principle. Jesus would have been taught the Golden Rule as a boy growing up in the Jewish tradition. Jesus' version of this teaching as we find it presented in the Gospels clearly shows how highly he regarded it:

> "In everything do to others as you would have them do to you; for this is the law and the prophets" (Matthew 7:12).

Right Livelihood

The Golden Rule should be a constant guideline for all of our interactions with other people including those involved in our means of earning a living. If we are an employee we should work for our employer in the same way we would want someone to work for us. If we are an employer we should treat our employees and customers in the same way we would want to be treated if our roles were reversed.

The essence of Right Livelihood in the Buddhist tradition is that our work should not cause harm to others, either directly or indirectly. We are also to avoid any deceitful, unethical business practices and any kind of exploitation. Today more than ever we are to be mindful that our work does not exploit or harm the environment. It is particularly important that people who work in government strive to live up to these ideals and ensure that regulatory measures are in place to protect citizens and the natural world.

Some people have the good fortune to know from an early age that they were meant to be a scientist, teacher, musician, or involved in some other profession. For the rest of us finding a career that suits our talents and contributes to our development and to society in a positive way is a more difficult process. We should not be judgmental in what constitutes a "good job." Thank God for the people who work to keep our world clean, or build the structures and equipment that enable people like doctors and scientists to do their work.

My own work history is replete with relatively low paying jobs that were physically demanding. While I may not have always enjoyed them at the time I can look back now and see how they helped me to learn the value of hard work, become more humble and less judgmental, and cultivate greater compassion for people in difficult situations. Every job that meets the criteria for Right Livelihood has value and can be beneficial to our development in some way.

Joseph Campbell used to advise people to "follow your bliss." This teaching is not about doing whatever gives you pleasure, it is about finding that pursuit that makes your eyes light up when you talk about it. It is about pursuing work and activities that allow us to express our innate Buddha nature, be productive, and feel more alive and vibrant.

The Buddhist tradition is very practical and many of its teachings provide common sense advice for living a happy and productive life. Lama Surya Das has written about a story that illustrates this point:

> "The Buddha once told the layman Dighajanu that there are four things conducive to happiness in this world: to be skilled, efficient, energetic, earnest, and learned in whatever profession one has; to conscientiously protect one's income and family's means of support; to have virtuous, trustworthy, and faithful friends and spiritual aspirations; to be content and to live within one's means."(10)

Right Effort

To make progress along the spiritual path takes a certain amount of determination and effort. It takes concentrated effort to break free from any negative patterns of thinking and acting that hold us back from moving forward and reaching the peak of our potential. It also takes discipline to constantly guard against developing any new negative patterns.

In the Islamic tradition the word *jihad*, meaning "striving, exertion," refers to this inner struggle against the egoic self as we make our way along the straight path to God. This internal fight between selfishness and selflessness is won with the slaying of the ego.

As we make progress in our spiritual practice our karmic loads become lighter and Right Effort begins to take on a quality of effortlessness. Actually, it is important that we come to the realization that it is not possible to reach the kingdom of God by relying on our own efforts. We need to learn to rely on our heart's connection to the unconditional Love from the Source of Love.

The advanced practitioner learns to "go with the flow" and becomes increasingly serene and calm. Our inner heart becomes our guide and life becomes an exciting adventure that is lived with a joyous equanimity. All of our daily activities become infused with spiritual meaning.

Right Mindfulness

Any previous mentions of "living in the present moment," or the need for "constant attention" and "increased awareness" were alluding to the need for Right Mindfulness. Mindfulness practice is extremely beneficial for training our minds and elevating our awareness. By consciously bringing our attention to our thoughts, words, and deeds we can break free of negative patterns and rise above conditioned thinking.

The famous saying attributed to Socrates, "The unexamined life is not worth living," speaks of the need to be mindful of every aspect of our lives. An unexamined life leads to unconscious living which results in negative karmic patterns being reinforced, and thoughts and behaviours that are detrimental to spiritual progress. In the words of Paul to those who would consider themselves to be a Christian: "Examine yourselves to see whether you are living in the faith" (2 Corinthians 13:5).

The primary focus of mindfulness practice is striving for mastery of our minds. Too often our attention is not on the task at hand. Instead of concentrating on (and fully enjoying and experiencing) whatever it is we are doing, we are thinking about something that happened in the past or some anticipated future event. Our physical bodies are in one place while our minds are somewhere else. Rumi once wrote that, "Past and future veil God from our sight."(11) When we fully experience the present moment we touch the eternal – here and now.

Buddhist teachers tell us that everyday activities are a wonderful opportunity to practice mindfulness. Use activities like ironing or doing the laundry to practice being fully present and not allowing the mind to wander to other things. When having a shower or bath try to clear your mind and allow yourself to experience the moment. Perhaps you might visualize the water as healing light that is cleansing your body of any impurities. While eating a meal we should be grateful for every bite and mindful to bring our full attention to experiencing the taste and texture of our food.

Ultimately we are practicing mindfulness as a means to make progress in breaking free of compulsive thinking. Eckhart Tolle has done a beautiful job of articulating the problem of unconscious identification with the mind and how the vast majority of people in this world are enslaved to incessant thinking. (12) Only in liberation from enslavement to our minds can we know true freedom.

Right Meditation

Meditation is one of the best spiritual tools we have for accelerating our spiritual evolution and becoming free of the egoic self and its influence on our thinking. Paramahansa Yogananda liked to say that "meditation is to religion what the laboratory is to science." Everyone should meditate regularly, regardless of their belief system. Even just five minutes of meditation a day has spiritual, mental, and physical benefits.

Ideally we should try and meditate at least thirty minutes a day, perhaps something like twenty minutes at night before going to bed and ten minutes in the morning. It is best to sit in a comfortable position where the spine is straight and the arms are relaxed. Prior to December 12, 2008 the focus of my meditative practice was to make progress in stilling my mind. I thought of it as striving to transcend the stormy waters of the conscious and subconscious minds and to enter into the perfect calm of the mind of Christ.

Like many people I would begin a session by focusing on my breath. Breathe in deeply, breathe out deeply. If the mind wanders draw it back into your breathing. Feel the diaphragm rise and lower while the lungs expand and contract. Relax deeply, while letting go of any tension in your body. Be in the moment.

Being an analytical thinker by nature I found it difficult to let myself go and not think about the process. I found the use of visualization to be helpful. I would visualize a body of water (that I thought of as the subconscious) rippling with waves and then see these waves dissipate until the water was perfectly still like a sheet of glass. While visualizing this scene I would be telling myself "Peace be still."

A short time into my meditative practice I began using "white light" visualizations. I would visualize a white light entering the top of my head until my entire body was filled with light. I would see any negative energies or worries being dissolved in this healing light. Then I would visualize every brain cell shining with light, my mind being illumined, and all human density and ignorance evaporating in the light. Often while visualizing this mental illumination I would pray "let that mind be in me which was in Christ Jesus."

After a couple of years of practice I began to make progress in stilling the mind and experiencing deep meditation. As I have said earlier, I became aware of periods of no-thought that would gradually grow in length and depth. This is a common and natural result of a sustained meditative practice. This is in fact the beginning of an awakening or restoration to our natural state of mind, sometimes called original mind or big mind.

The small mind (or monkey mind) with its deluded and compulsive thinking begins to lose its grip, so to speak. The Buddha within begins to awaken and our thinking increases in clarity as we increasingly become able to see things as they are. Our level of awareness rises above the small mind and propels us into a new mode of being.

After December of 2008 the focus of my meditative practice was on feeling God's Love and enjoying the feeling of being loved so deeply and completely. This type of meditation could be called a heart meditation. Mental stillness is very nice, feeling God's Love work on and

through your whole heart and whole being is so beautiful...
it feels so good.

A heart meditation begins by sitting still with your
spine straight and saying a short prayer for the Love to help
you to relax and feel the Love. Then close your eyes and
touch your heart to help reduce the activity of your brain
and bring your attention to your heart center. Then do
nothing...just relax and feel the Love flowing...into the top
of your head and throughout your whole body...and enjoy
the beautiful feeling...and be grateful.

With regular periods of deep meditation we can make
strides in purifying our mind of past conditioning. Mental
and emotional energetic blockages can be dissolved in
the Love. The benefits derived from the consistent use of
meditation are many. Besides increased feelings of peace
and serenity along with greater mental clarity we also find
that our prayer life becomes enhanced. Meister Eckhart
(1260-1327), the often quoted Dominican priest and mystic,
believed that the most powerful prayer was the outcome of
a quiet mind.

The Power of Prayer

To this point this writing has probably made the process
of spiritual transformation sound somewhat daunting, but
there is help available to us. We do not have to make the
journey on our own with just the guidance of a few teachers
along the way. There is such a thing as grace. Prayer is the
wonderful means we have of talking to the One Who Loves

us the most, whether it be in forms of structured prayer or simply thoughts we have throughout the day.

There is no denying the power of the spoken word, so when possible we should try to pray out loud. Obviously there are times when it is not appropriate to verbalize prayer, but we should never doubt the power of "thoughtful" prayers, especially if they are spontaneous and come from the heart.

One of the most powerful responses to prayer that I have experienced (that I was quickly aware of) came from a short, thoughtful prayer. One morning while working at a grocery store, many years ago, I was unloading a shipment of pallets and everything seemed to be going badly. On top of the problems we were having with the shipment I felt very tired and the truck driver was half asleep himself from working a second job the previous night. At one point because of his condition he nearly crushed me in between two pallets of stock. Thankfully, instead of getting angry with him I closed my eyes and prayed "God, please help me to find the strength to get through this day." I never could have imagined the powerful effect this little prayer would have on me. Within minutes I felt myself being filled with a loving energy which stayed with me throughout a remarkably productive day.

Following the advice of the Edgar Cayce material I frequently pray: "Your will O God, not mine but Thine be done, in me – through me." Another little prayer that I have used often through the years was inspired by Saint Francis of Assisi and goes, "Lord, make me an instrument of your peace and love in this world." The Lord's Prayer and Psalm

23 have also been a source of comfort to me since the early days of my prayer life.

Intercessory prayer should take up a significant portion of our prayer life. Everyone should try to develop the habit of not only praying for family and people in trouble throughout the world, but also for people who may just briefly catch our eye in our daily lives. One example of this from my life is when someone cuts me off in traffic I like to say a prayer for them. I pray that whatever caused them to drive recklessly will be resolved and that they will be mindful of driving more safely in the future. We should try to be constantly sending out positive vibrations to others with short prayers or positive thoughts for them.

Paul taught that we should "pray without ceasing" (1 Thessalonians 5:17). The Greek word for "without ceasing" actually means constantly recurring. It is important to use prayer regularly in every aspect of our life. When we are practicing mindfulness or meditating it is especially important. If we do not include prayer with these practices we are in danger of becoming detached and aloof with a desire to "rise above it all."

If we are only a detached observer we will not be in our hearts. When we observe a negative tendency coming to the surface (in my experience the workplace provides many opportunities for this to happen) we should always say a short prayer for True Source Love to help us to remove this tendency from our hearts and minds.

Heartfelt prayer helps us to feel, enjoy, and accept God's Love for us. A prayerful life helps keep our hearts directed towards God and to live our lives from within the Love. It is possible for the field of our spiritual heart to grow so large that we can feel like we are walking around within a bubble of love.

While first reading "The Imitation of Christ" I highlighted the sentences which jumped out at me as I do with every spiritual book I read. In later re-reading the sentences which were highlighted in one of the chapters I realized that put together they would become a beautiful prayer. Here are those words:

> "O Lord, in simplicity of heart I offer myself to you this day, to be your servant for ever: I do this as an act of homage to You, and as an act of perpetual praise...Lord, I offer on Your altar of reconciliation all the sins and offences that I have ever committed before You and Your holy Angels, from the day of my first sin until now, praying You to burn them in the fire of Your love...I commit myself entirely to Your mercy, and resign myself into Your hands...I offer to You also whatever is good in me...that You may strengthen and hallow it...and raise it continually towards perfection...I offer You also all the holy aspirations of devout persons...I pray that all these may enjoy the assistance of Your grace, the aid of Your comfort, protection from dangers, and deliverance from pains to come; and that, freed from all evils, they may offer glad praise and thanks to You...O Lord, take from our hearts all suspicion, ill-feeling, anger, and contention, and whatever may injure charity and brotherly love. Have mercy, O Lord, have mercy on all who ask Your mercy. Give grace to those who sorely need it; and help us all

so to live that we may worthily enjoy Your grace,
and finally come to everlasting life."(13) Amen.

Prayer is also an important part of the spiritual life of most Buddhists. Lama Surya Das has said that he likes to start his day with a prayer derived from a Buddhist scripture called the Metta Sutra. Here is the wonderful Metta Prayer:

May all beings be happy, content, and fulfilled.

May all beings be healed and whole.

May all have whatever they want and need.

May all be protected from harm, and free from fear.

May all beings enjoy inner peace and ease.

May all be awakened, liberated, and free.

May there be peace in this world, and throughout the entire universe. (14)

With prayer and meditation we open ourselves up to the Source of life and allow God's Love to flow to us. By doing this we are renewed in every possible way which can lead to spiritual awakenings and transformations of consciousness. Awakening to the reality that the love and compassion of a Buddha is our true nature and understanding the oneness of all life are keys to positive change. This indwelling

Buddha, this Christ within, is waiting to be formed in us and fill us with love.

Peace and Love

Religion should provide us with instructions on how to purify the heart and mind. The focus of much of this writing has been on purifying and transforming the mind. Cognitive development and a clear mind are very important but nothing is more important than love. God's Love is the only cleansing agent for purifying our spiritual heart. The message of Jesus was centered in love and the need for us to love one another.

> "You shall love the Lord your God with all your heart, and with all your soul, and with all your mind" (Matthew 22:37).

> "You shall love your neighbour as yourself" (Matthew 22:39).

> "Love one another as I have loved you" (John 15:12).

The teachings of Jesus can bring us to the presence of Love. With Paul we can reach the point where we can say that "God's love has been poured into our hearts through the Holy Spirit" (Romans 5:5). We learn to live so that we do not block the flow of God's Love to us or to be a stumbling block in the path of another.

Our heart is the key to growing spiritually. Christ consciousness may be the way to the Kingdom of God but a clean spiritual heart is the key needed to unlock the door to the Kingdom. "Blessed are the pure in heart, for they will see God," says Jesus (Matthew 5:8).

God loves us completely and unconditionally every moment, and wants nothing more than to cleanse our hearts and bring us Home. But we have free will and we need to ask for help...we need to pray for God's Love to cleanse our hearts. We need to pray often for help in letting go and being free of the many ways that we limit God's Love for us.

For most of us our direct love connection with our Source is nowhere near what it could be because our hearts are not open enough and are clogged with negativities. We are solely responsible for this "clogging of the arteries" of our spiritual hearts. These negativities are byproducts of our own emotional/egoic reactivity (reactions based in fear, anger, judgment, etc.). It is not what happens to us in our lives that leads to a less than pure heart but how we react to what happens to us.

While it would be nice if we never reacted with emotions like anger, when we do we can always pray. A little prayer something like "True Source, please bless my heart so that all anger and related negative energy be cleansed...be removed...to be replaced with Your Love...Thank You True Source...Amen" can work wonders and help to keep our hearts clean.

Our spiritual heart is the center of all beautiful feelings like peace, joy, and love. When our hearts are touched in some way and we feel an expansive, light feeling in our chest area this is the result of our non-physical heart opening and expanding.

Be still...close your eyes...relax...smile...feel your heart... smile sweetly and freely to your heart...feel the love that is flowing continuously to your heart...and be grateful to True Source...now feel the love radiating from your heart... sharing the love with everyone that you meet and with every being...

"Whenever you stand praying, forgive, if you have anything against anyone; so that your Father in heaven may also forgive you your trespasses" (Mark 11:25). One of the most common ways we block the flow of love to us is by stubbornly refusing to forgive...others and ourselves. To forgive does not mean we have to condone whatever has caused the hurtful feelings. However, by holding on to feelings of bitterness and resentment we ultimately damage our own well-being.

"Do not worry about anything, but in everything by prayer and supplication with thanksgiving let your requests be made known to God" (Philippians 4:6). I truly believe that many people worry themselves sick...literally. I do not understand what sitting around and worrying about a person or situation does to help that person or situation. Do not waste your energy by pouring it into feelings of worry. Why worry when you can pray?

In a discussion with his disciples regarding who is great in the kingdom of heaven Jesus brought forth a small child and said, "Truly I tell you, unless you become like children, you will never enter the kingdom of heaven. Whoever becomes humble like this child is the greatest in the kingdom of heaven" (Matthew 18:1-4). This startling teaching points to the need for purity of heart and mind and the importance of being humble.

"Love your enemies and pray for those who persecute you" (Matthew 5:44). Can we move beyond forgiving those we feel have hurt us in some way to loving and praying for them? This is what Jesus asks us to do. Love has the power to transform even the most difficult situations into opportunities for growth and increased awareness.

Living the teachings of Jesus helps us to feel God's Love for us more fully. Awareness of the developmental process and understanding the role the ego plays in people's lives should move us towards compassion. As much as possible strive to bring the presence of Love into your life and everyday situations. It is especially important to try and be mindful of doing this when dealing with people who "push your buttons."

Compassionate understanding should result from awareness of the fact that when someone hurts us in some way they are acting from a place of pain within themselves. If we consistently bring love and compassion to a difficult situation or relationship of some kind we will eventually transform that situation or relationship in a positive way. By consciously choosing not to react in a negative fashion to the egoic ways of others the cycle of egoic reactivity is broken and an opening emerges for healing and transformation.

With this increase in awareness we are less prone to judging people because we now have some understanding of what was behind their actions or words. Becoming less judgmental and more compassionate is a sure sign of spiritual growth. In the words of Jesus:

"Do not judge, so that you may not be
judged. For with the judgement you make you
will be judged, and the measure you give will be
the measure you get. Why do you see the speck
in your neighbor's eye, but do not notice the log
in your own eye?" (Matthew 7:1-3).

Peace and love, purifying the mind and heart, and the
teachings of the Buddha and the Christ all complement
one another in a beautiful way. Generally speaking, men
have a tendency to focus on the mind while women have
more of a tendency to focus on the heart. This is one of the
reasons women generally have a greater inclination towards
spirituality and sacrificial giving. Again, it is crucial that
the roles of the masculine and the feminine come into
balance in this world. The world's religions will become
less and less relevant to people's spiritual lives unless they
evolve and women have equal opportunity for leadership
roles.

Once we reach the rational and vision-logic levels of
consciousness we should begin to see clearly how things
like sexism, racism, and religious conflict are the products
of ignorance. And as our understanding becomes deeper
we realize that our current physical form is nothing but a
temporary vehicle for our souls and spirits to use for the
purpose of playing a new role on Earth's stage. Underneath
our physical form we are in essence spiritual beings with
"spiritual bodies" that are not male or female. Our spiritual
bodies do not have skin, much less skin colour.

Likewise when we die and shed these "coats of skin"
we will not be Christian, Buddhist, Muslim or whatever
the case may be. Therefore it is clear that salvation is not

found by becoming a Christian, Buddhist, or Muslim. We are saved by believing in God's Love for us and letting it help us to become born anew...to become clean again...to awaken to our true self having learned what we needed to learn...having realized what we needed to realize.

Religions have emerged at different times across different cultures as organized expressions of the teachings of extraordinary individuals who were able to express that possibility in a powerful way.

Unfortunately religious organizations have had a tendency to become dysfunctional as egos clash and to degenerate into idolatry. This idolatry continues to be prevalent in every tradition, including the monotheistic religions. Here we are speaking of the worship of the founding figures, the worship of holy books, and a kind of worship of the religious tradition itself.

Draw near to God's consciousness and the presence of Love will draw near to you. Those with a clear mind and a pure heart will see that the egoic sense of self is nothing but an illusion and they will see the God beyond mythic conceptions of God.

Religion that is pure and worthwhile results in charitable works, the sacrificing of oneself for another. And reaching true self-realization where God's peace and love dwells in us bodily requires the sacrifice of one's self to God. Are you willing to lose your self to find your true self? Are you ready to break free from the control of the ego and enslavement to compulsive thinking? Many are called to do what it takes to reach this point, but few are willing to make the necessary sacrifices. Are you?

Jesus taught us that:

> "If any want to become my followers, let them deny themselves and take up their own cross and follow me. For those who want to save their life will lose it, and those who lose their life for my sake will find it" (Matthew 16:24-25).

And near the end of the *Bhagavad Gita* the Lord says:

> "Hear again my Word supreme, the deepest secret of all. Because I love you, I will speak to you words of salvation. Give your mind to me, and give me your heart, and your sacrifice, and your adoration. This is my Word of promise: you shall surely come to me, for you are precious to me. Leave all things behind, and come to me for your salvation. I will make you free from the bondage of sin. Fear no more." (18:64-66)

"Blessed are those who hunger and thirst for righteousness, for they will be filled" says Jesus (Matthew 5:6). May the stream of your life flow into the river of righteousness, and may God's peace and Love be with you always.

Afterword

An open and clean spiritual heart is vital to our spiritual health. The good news is that we have reached a point where collectively enough people have let the Love help them to open their hearts that spiritual growth can happen much more quickly and easily than in the past. And the more we realize that growing spiritually is meant to be a natural, effortless process where we whole-heartedly accept God's Love and help, our collective spiritual evolution will continue to accelerate.

Many of us have had the tendency to be too intense...too serious..too reliant on our own efforts or intentions...and too dominated by our mind with its complex, theological concepts. When we learn to shift our attention from our minds to our hearts we see that what is good for our heart is really quite simple. Being relaxed...smiling...a heartfelt hug...a simple prayer...these are the types of things that make our hearts happy and healthy.

If you feel you would like to learn more about the spiritual heart and how to let your inner heart be your guide please consider reading *Smile to your Heart Meditations* by Irmansyah Effendi and *The Way of the Spiritual Heart* by Ed Rubenstein. These books will help you greatly.

Thank you to all who have been helpful to my spiritual life over these past thirty years, including in the publication of this book. And a special thanks to all the beautiful hearts who have helped me to learn more about the spiritual heart from 2009 to the present. And finally, thank you to my wife Rosana for being so understanding and supportive. I love you sweetheart.

Endnotes

Part 1

The quote on the title page is from *The Power of Myth*, page 206.

1   Malachi 4:5
2   Betty J. Eadie, *Embraced by the Light*, p. 29-30.
3   Raymond A. Moody, *Life after Life*, p. 65.
4   Dannion Brinkley, *Saved by the Light*, p. 20-21.
5   Kenneth Ring, *Heading towards Omega*, p. 162.
6   W. D. Davies, *Jewish and Pauline Studies*, p. 166.
7   The four Gospels are usually dated between 65 and 100 CE. Almost all scholars agree that the Letter to the Hebrews was not written by Paul. The author of this unusual piece of writing is unknown, and it is usually thought to have been produced in the early second century.
8   Burton Mack, *Who Wrote the New Testament?*, p.103.
9   Daniel Boyarin, *A Radical Jew*, p. 7.
10 Ibid., p. 54.
11 Ibid., p. 110-111
12 Gershom Scholem, *Kabbalah*, p. 345.

13 Gershom Scholem, *On the Mystical Shape of the Godhead*, p. 200.

14 Ibid., p. 228.

15 Lawrence Fine, *Safed Spirituality*, p. 24.

16 Ibid., p. 61.

17 Ibid., p. 63.

18 Wouter Hanegraaff, *New Age Religion and Western Culture*, p. 388.

19 Ibid., p. 449-452.

20 Ibid., p. 453.

21 Mary Pat Fisher, *Living Religions*, p. 352.

22 Huston Smith, *World's Religions*, p. 63.

23 Ibid., p. 68.

24 Roger Walsh, *Essential Spirituality*, p. 40.

25 Thich Nhat Hanh, *Living Buddha, Living Christ*, p. 136.

26 Paramahansa Yogananda, *Whispers from Eternity*, p. 24.

27 Juan Mascaro, *The Bhagavad Gita*, p. 85.

28 Aldous Huxley, *The Perennial Philosophy*, p. 21.

29 Ibid., p. 23.

30 Eric J. Sharpe, *Comparative Religion a History*, p. 35.

31 Russell T. McCutcheon, *Critics not Caretakers*, p. x.

32 Ibid., p. x-xi.

33 William E. Paden, *Interpreting the Sacred*, p. 28. This little book is a very good overview of different ways of viewing religion. It is a rare jewel among books written by Religious Studies academics in that it is written in a concise, readable manner.

34 Ring, p. 84-85.

35 Larsen, p. 549.

36 Ken Wilber, *A Theory of Everything*, p. 84.

37 Wilber, *The Marriage of Sense and Soul*, p. 6.

38 Ibid., p. 9.

39 John Haught, *Science and Religion*, p. 98.

40 Ibid., p. 98.

41 Ibid., p. 43.

42 Ibid., p. 67.

43 Eckhart Tolle, *A New Earth*, p. 96.

44 Ibid., p. 109.

Part 2

The quote on the title page is found in *Essential Spirituality*, page 22.

1 Marion, *Putting on the Mind of Christ*, p.29.

2 Marion, *The Death of the Mythic God*, p. 4.

3 Marion, *Putting on the Mind of Christ*, p. 37.

4 Marion, *The Death of the Mythic God*, p. 5-6.

5 Ibid., p. 6.

6 Ibid., p. 6.

7 Ibid., p. 6.

8 Ibid., p. 10.

9 Ibid., p. 10.

10 Ibid., p. 9.

11 Campbell, *Thou Art That*, p. 1-2.

12 Moody, *The Light Beyond*, p. 49.

13 Marion, *Putting on the Mind of Christ*, p. 55.

14 Neil Postman, *Technopoly*, p. 37.

15 The Britannica Guide to *The Ideas that made the Modern World*, p. 227.

16 Marion, *The Death of the Mythic God*, p. 95.

17 Ibid., p. 102.
18 Marion, *Putting on the Mind of Christ*, p. 63.
19 Sharpe, p. 31.
20 Hanegraaff, p. 448.
21 Marion, *Putting on the Mind of Christ*, p. 65.
22 Wilber, *A Sociable God*, p. 38.
23 Marion, *The Death of the Mythic God*, p. 116.
24 Caroline Myss, *Anatomy of the Spirit*, p. 67.
25 Marion, *The Death of the Mythic God*, p. 119.
26 Max Jammer, *Einstein and Religion*, p. 39-40.
27 Ibid., p. 32.
28 Marion, *Putting on the Mind of Christ*, p. 113.
29 Ibid., p. 183.
30 Ibid., p. 213.
31 Ibid., p. 208.
32 Ibid., p. 208.
33 Wilber, *A Brief History of Everything*, p. 67.
34 Ibid., p. 67.

Part 3

The quote on the title page is a popular rendition of a Confucian teaching.

1 Campbell, *Thou Art That*, p. 12-13.
2 Walsh, p. 214.
3 Marion, *The Death of the Mythic God*, p. 142.
4 Walsh, p. 79.
5 Lama Surya Das, p. 173.
6 Thomas a Kempis, *The Imitation of Christ*, p. 37.
7 As quoted in Walsh, p. 226.

8   Lama Surya Das, p. 198.

9   Ibid., p. 223-224.

10 Ibid., p. 233.

11 Huxley, p. 188.

12 Tolle, *The Power of Now*, p. 14-21.

13 *The Imitation of Christ*, p. 199-201.

14 Lama Surya Das, p. 183-184.

Bibliography

Boyarin, Daniel. *A Radical Jew: Paul and the Politics of Identity.* University of California Press, 1994.

Brinkley, Dannion (with Paul Perry). *Saved by the Light.* New York: Villard Books, 1994.

Campbell, Joseph. (Betty Sue Flowers, Ed.) *The Power of Myth.* Anchor Books Edition, 1991.

_____. (Eugene Kennedy, Ed.) *Thou Art That.* New World Library, 2001.

Davies, W. D. *Jewish and Pauline Studies.* Philadelphia: Fortress Press, 1984.

Drummond, Richard Henry. *A Life of Jesus the Christ.* St. Martin's Paperbacks edition, 1996.

Eadie, Betty. *Embraced by the Light.* Bantam edition, 1994.

Effendi, Irmansyah. *Smile to your Heart Meditations.* Ulysses Press, 2010.

_____. *The Real You: Beyond Forms and Lives.* Balboa Press, 2012.

_____. *Spirituality: The Meaning, Our Journey and the True Path.* Natural Way of Living, 2018.

Ehrman, Bart. *The New Testament: A Historical Introduction to the Early Christian Writings.* Oxford University Press, 1997.

Eisenman, Robert. *James the Brother of Jesus.* New York: Penguin Books, 1997.

Fine, Lawrence. *Safed Spirituality.* New York: Paulist Press, 1984.

Fisher, Mary Pat. *Living Religions.* Prentice Hall, 1997.

Godman, David (Ed.) *Be As You Are: The Teachings of Sri Ramana Maharshi.* Penguin Books, 1992.

Hanegraaff, Wouter J. *New Age Religion and Western Culture.* State University of New York Press, 1998.

Hanh, Thich Nhat. *Peace Is Every Step.* Bantam Books, 1992.

_____. *Living Buddha, Living Christ.* Riverhead Books, 1995.

Harvey, Andrew. (Ed.) *The Essential Mystics.* San Francisco, 1996.

Haught, John F. *Science & Religion: From Conflict to Conversation.* New York: Paulist Press, 1995.

Huxley, Aldous. (1945). *The Perennial Philosophy*. Harper & Row, Harper Colophon edition, 1970.

Jammer, Max. *Einstein and Religion*. Princeton University Press, 1999.

Kempis, Thomas. (Leo Shirley-Price, Trans.) *The Imitation of Christ*. Penguin Books, 1952.

Lafargue, Michael. (Trans.) *The Tao of the Tao Te Ching*. State University of New York Press, 1992.

Lama Surya Das. *Awakening the Buddha Within*. New York: Broadway Books, 1997.

Larsen, Stephen and Robin. (1991). *Joseph Campbell: A Fire in the Mind*. Inner Traditions, 2002.

Mack, Burton. *Who Wrote the New Testament?* New York: Harper Collins, 1995.

Marion, Jim. *Putting on the Mind of Christ*. Hampton Roads, 2000.

_____. *The Death of the Mythic God: The Rise of Evolutionary Spirituality*. Hampton Roads, 2004.

McCutcheon, Russell T. *Critics not Caretakers*. State University of New York Press, 2001.

Moody, Raymond. *Life after Life*. New York: Bantam, 1976.

_____. *The Light Beyond*. New York: Bantam, 1988.

Muggeridge, Malcolm. (1971) *Something Beautiful for God.* Harper&Row Paperback edition, 1986.

Myss, Caroline. *Anatomy of the Spirit.* New York: Harmony Books, 1996.

Nasr, Seyyed Hossein. *The Garden of Truth.* New York: HarperCollins, 2007.

Newton, Michael. *Journey of Souls.* Llewellyn Publications, 1996.

_____. *Destiny of Souls.* Llewellyn Publications, 2000.

Paden, William E. *Interpreting the Sacred.* Boston: Beacon Press, 1992.

Pagels, Elaine. *The Gnostic Gospels.* New York: Vintage Books, 1979.

Peale, Norman Vincent. (1952). *The Power of Positive Thinking.* New York: Fawcett Crest edition, 1987.

Pennachio, John. "Near-Death Experience as Mystical Experience." *Journal of Religion and Health,* Vol.25, no.1 (spr. 1986), p. 64-72.

Postman, Neil. *Technopoly.* New York: Vintage Books, 1993.

Ring, Kenneth. *Heading Towards Omega: In Search of the Meaning of the NDE.* New York: William Morrow, 1984.

Robinson, James M. (Ed.) (1978) *The Nag Hammadi Library.* HarperCollins Paperback edition, 1990.

Rubenstein, Ed. *The Way of the Spiritual Heart.* LotusHeart Publishing, 2012.

Scholem, Gershom. (1974) *Kabbalah.* New York: Dorset Press, 1987.

_____. *On the Mystical Shape of the Godhead.* New York: Schocken, 1991.

Sharpe, Eric J. (1975) *Comparative Religion: A History.* Open Court printing, 1997.

Smith, Huston. (1958). *The Illustrated World's Religions.* HarperSanFrancisco edition, 1994.

Stearn, Jess. *Edgar Cayce - The Sleeping Prophet.* New York: Doubleday & Co., 1967.

The Britannica Guide to *The Ideas That Made The Modern World.* Robinson and Britannica, 2008.

Tolle, Eckhart. (1999). *The Power of Now.* New World Library and Namaste Publishing edition, 2004.

_____. *A New Earth.* First Plume printing, 2006.

Walsh, Roger. *Essential Spirituality.* John Wiley & Sons Inc., 1999.

Wilber, Ken. (1983). *A Sociable God: Toward a New Understanding of Religion.* Boston & London: Shambhala Publications, 2005.

_____. *A Brief History of Everything.* Boston & London: Shambhala Publications, 1996.

_____. *The Marriage of Sense and Soul: Integrating Science and Religion.* New York: Broadway Books, 1999.

_____. *A Theory of Everything.* Boston: Shambhala Publications, 2000.

Yogananda, Paramahansa. (1946). *Autobiography of a Yogi.* Self-Realization Fellowship, Twelfth edition, 1993.

_____. (1949). *Whispers from Eternity.* Self-Realization Fellowship, Ninth edition, 1992.